In 2001, join the BBC Proms on a musical odyssey.

Music and Pastoral The countryside has inspired composers across the centuries: from Handel setting Milton's *L'Allegro*, Haydn portraying the colours of *The Seasons* and Beethoven evoking nature in his *Pastoral Symphony*, through to Vaughan Williams's *Pastoral Symphony* with its echoes of war and Tippett's vision of *The Rose Lake*. Sally Beamish and James MacMillan write new works around topical pastoral and environmental themes.

Music in Exile Follow the fate of Schoenberg (who died 50 years ago) and other émigré composers who, in escaping Europe for America, were 'exiled to Paradise'. Bartók wrote his *Concerto for Orchestra* and Martinů wrote his Sixth Symphony for the Boston Symphony and Koussevitzky (who also died 50 years ago), Rakhmaninov composed his *Symphonic Dances* in the USA, while on the West Coast Stravinsky turned to the symphony and Schoenberg wrote *A Survivor from Warsaw*. Verdi's homesick Hebrew slaves and the sounds of Klezmer and Gypsy music also reflect the world of the dispossessed.

Leonard Slatkin arrives as the BBC Symphony Orchestra's new Chief Conductor, exploring the links between Britain and America in music by John Adams, Vaughan Williams and Benjamin Britten (another European émigré to America), as well as conducting new works by Christopher Rouse and Alexander Goehr, and a big-band late-night event. He is joined by many leading conductors: Bernard Haitink with the Boston Symphony and Daniel Barenboim with the Chicago; Günter Wand in Bruckner, Simon Rattle in Beethoven; Vladimir Ashkenazy with the Czech Philharmonic and Herbert Blomstedt with the Leipzig Gewandhaus; Christoph Eschenbach, Thomas Dausgaard and Antonio Pappano all making their Proms debuts.

Verdi's centenary is marked, English music is explored with the anniversaries of Gerald Finzi and Edmund Rubbra (both born 1901) and Constant Lambert (died 1951), while music from Stanley Kubrick's film *2001: A Space Odyssey* is threaded through the season.

Broadcasting brings the Proms to millions. Every Prom is broadcast on Radio 3 and streamed online, and more Proms than ever before are being televised, including a whole week of them on BBC Knowledge. So see you there! Or, if you can't attend, why not listen in, watch or log on!

Nicholas Kenyon

Nicholas Kenyon, Director, BBC Proms

Contents

The BBC presents the 107th season of Henry Wood Promenade Concerts

Royal Albert Hall, London

20 July – 15 September 2001

Your Guide to the Proms

How to Book

The BBC Proms: a continuing history of innovation ....

The Proms were founded to bring the best of classical music to a wide audience in an informal setting. From the outset, part of the audience has always stood in the 'promenade'. Prom places originally cost just a shilling; today, standing places at the Royal Albert Hall still cost only £3.00, and over 1,000 tickets go on sale for every concert from an hour before. Programmes have always mixed the great classics with what Henry Wood, the first conductor of the Proms, called his 'novelties' – rare works and premieres.

1895 The 26-year-old Henry Wood launches the Promenade Concerts at the newly opened Queen's Hall in Langham Place, close to where BBC Broadcasting House now stands. Wood goes on to conduct the Proms throughout their first 50 years. **1905** Wood composes his celebrated *Fantasia on British Sea-Songs* for a special Trafalgar Day concert: it proves so popular that it has been repeated at almost every Last Night ever since. **1927** The BBC takes over the running of the Proms; its own orchestras now provide the backbone of the season. **1941** The Proms move to the Royal Albert Hall after the Queen's Hall is gutted in a German air raid. **1942** The BBC SO shares the season for the first time with another orchestra, the LPO. **1944** Henry Wood dies shortly after celebrating his Proms jubilee. **1947** The Last Night is seen on TV for the first time. **1950** Malcolm Sargent becomes Chief Conductor of the BBC SO. **1953** The first out-of-London orchestra appears at the Proms: the Hallé, from Manchester, under John Barbirolli. **1955** First Proms visit by the National Youth Orchestra. **1960** First BBC Proms commission: William Alwyn's *Derby Day*. First electronic piece heard at the Proms: Berio's *Perspectives*. **1961** First complete opera to be given at the Proms: Mozart's *Don Giovanni*, brought by Glyndebourne. **1966** First foreign orchestra to play at the Proms: the Moscow Radio Orchestra, under Gennady Rozhdestvensky. **1967** Colin Davis becomes Chief Conductor of the BBC SO. **1968** As the First

Night moves from Saturday to Friday, Messiaen's *La transfiguration* inaugurates a new tradition of single-work openings. **1970** The first Late Night Prom features cult pop group The Soft Machine. **1971** First world music to be heard at the Proms: a sitar recital by Imrat Khan. Pierre Boulez becomes Chief Conductor of the BBC SO. **1974** First Pre-Prom Talks. First brass-band concert at the Proms, given by the combined Black Dyke Mills and Grimethorpe Colliery bands. **1989** Andrew Davis becomes Chief Conductor of the BBC SO. **1994** The Proms celebrate their 100th season with a season of past premieres. **1995** The Proms celebrate their centenary year with a season of new commissions. **1996** Launch of Proms in the Park, Proms Chamber Music and the Proms Lecture. **1997** Evgeny Kissin gives the first Proms solo recital. **2000** Launch of Poetry Proms at the Serpentine Gallery. Relaunch of the multi-work First Night. **2001** Leonard Slatkin becomes Chief Conductor of the BBC SO.

The BBC: bringing the Proms into your home

The Proms are accessible to all through BBC Radio 3 and BBC television broadcasts, and now you can hear them through the BBC's website too

The Proms on Radio 3 All 73 Proms will be broadcast live on BBC Radio 3 and many will also be rebroadcast on weekday afternoons. Proms Chamber Music concerts and Proms Composer Portraits will also all be broadcast live, while Poetry Proms and Performing Art talks will be recorded and broadcast as interval features during Proms relays on Tuesday and Thursday evenings.

The Proms on TV Six Proms will this year be shown live on BBC2, while five more will be recorded and shown on BBC1. A further eight will be shown, either live or recorded, on the BBC's new digital TV channel, BBC Knowledge.

The Proms Online All Proms are also streamed live via the BBC's website at **www.bbc.co.uk/proms**

www.bbc.co.uk/proms

AUGUSTUS
GENOVA

Exiled to Paradise

Following a century of unparalleled upheaval, Calum MacDonald charts the trans-continental wanderings of composers who were forced to find new songs to sing in strange lands

'The Americans expect great things of me. I am to show them the way into the Promised Land': Dvořák conducting at the World's Columbian Exposition in Chicago in 1893

LEFT
The New York skyline in 1931 as seen from an arriving ship

RIGHT
'How shall we sing the Lord's song in a strange land?': Psalm 137, the lament of the Jews in their Babylonian exile, by Eduard Bendemann (1811–89)

For Judaeo-Christian culture at least, the captivity of the Israelites in Babylon has been the very archetype of exile. Displaced, stateless, sundered from home and familiar surroundings, they find their old songs have lost their meaning. They must fashion new ones, appropriate to their situation: songs of lament, of longing for home, eventually of triumph over their oppressors. Their situation is poignantly evoked in Verdi's biblical opera *Nabucco*, most famously in the so-called Chorus of the Hebrew Slaves ('Va, pensiero') at the end of Act 3.

Exile, whether through enforced or voluntary emigration, is an age-old experience, one of the great human themes. For creative artists from Ovid (banished by the emperor Augustus to the Black Sea) to Mandelstam (confined by Stalin in Voronezh), exile brings not only pain and trauma but a profound shift in perspective, the urgent reordering of priorities. The old tradition of 'home thoughts from abroad' takes on a keener edge. At the end of the 19th century a teaching contract in America could provide Dvořák with the occasion to write a symphony 'From the New

World' full of nostalgia for the music and countryside of his native Bohemia. But there was no such freedom of choice for the millions who endured exile during the wars, the persecutions, the genocides of the 20th century. Creative artists shared in the rhythm of exodus and exile and, in their different ways, gave it expression. For the strongest, exile marked a new stage not just in their lives, but in their art as well.

Many of the works in this year's BBC Proms season illustrate that theme, especially in relation to two great political convulsions which caused successive waves of people to seek safety

beyond the borders of their homelands: the Russian Revolution of 1917, and the Fascist seizures of power across Europe, leading to the Second World War. Totalitarian regimes seek to crush dissent, wherever it may be suspected in the persons and especially the minds of their citizens: the time-honoured methods range from state murder to the burning of books and the banning of musical styles deemed 'degenerate' or inimical to the national health. Composers of independent and exploratory ideas were naturally in the firing line.

Rakhmaninov, Prokofiev and Stravinsky were three of the most prominent musicians to escape the new order in Russia. Stravinsky had already been living in neutral Switzerland since shortly after the outbreak of the First World War. Prokofiev would eventually tire of his rootless existence as an international composer-pianist and return to Russia in the 1930s, losing

Sergey Rakhmaninov (1873–1943)

Rhapsody on a Theme of Paganini
Prom 42

Symphonic Dances
Prom 57

Rakhmaninov wrote comparatively few works after he settled in the USA in the aftermath of the Russian Revolution, but it's arguable that those few include his finest achievements in the realm of concerto and symphony. With the *Rhapsody on a Theme of Paganini* he created one of the classic variation works in the repertoire – and, by turning Paganini's theme upside down, one of his own most instantly recognisable melodies. In the *Symphonic Dances* he came nearest to an accommodation with the modern spirit, while still remaining intensely Russian in character. Both works make use of the 'Dies irae' chant, the plainsong melody of which haunted him all his life.

some of his artistic independence in the process, however ingeniously he tried to preserve it. Rakhmaninov, the eldest, was very much a symbol of Tsarist days, but his music – now given a new focus for its already endemic nostalgia – continued developing on its own terms. Stravinsky went on to become the leader of the chic new neo-Classical style centred on Paris and on Diaghilev's dance company, the Ballets Russes, which was itself now a team of exiles.

Stravinsky and his compatriots were destined soon to be doubly exiled. With the rise of Hitler, Western Europe proved only a temporary sanctuary, and they became part of a second and yet larger wave of composer-refugees, forced to uproot themselves and seek safety across the sea, in Britain or (more often) in the USA. Although the largest element in this new diaspora was Jewish, typified by such prominent

Jewish musicians as Schoenberg, Zemlinsky, Milhaud and Weill, many non-Jews – such as Hindemith, Bartók and Martinů – also found themselves in opposition to, and in danger from, Fascism and took flight as well.

As Schoenberg once put it (ironically), they were all 'exiled to Paradise', forced to find their feet in an unfamiliarly rich, consumerist America, where the language was strange and they had to find what jobs they could. In fact, several found top academic professorships, since they were well-qualified – but at the price of resentment that this new influx of European talent was crowding out native US composers.

Sergey Prokofiev (1891–1953)

Piano Concerto No. 3
Prom 49

Although Prokofiev completed his Third Piano Concerto in Brittany in 1921, after leaving Russia because of the 1917 Revolution, most of his ideas for the piece had been accumulating during the war, and its Russian character is obvious. Indeed its vein of lyrical nostalgia is very different from the aggressive, spiky modernism of the music he had been writing for the past few years and it foreshadows the maturely balanced language of his later Soviet works. This concerto was the piece he played most on his first return visit to Russia in 1927, presaging his eventual permanent return from exile in 1933.

ABOVE
Prokofiev: a 1921 portrait
by Henri Matisse

LEFT
Rakhmaninov: the composer's
hands at the keyboard

ABOVE
'Bartók, the Mild-mannered Revolutionist': caricature of the composer at the piano by Aline Fruhauf (New York, 1927)

RIGHT
Stravinsky rehearsing at the BBC's Maida Vale Studios in 1958

Igor Stravinsky (1882–1971)
Symphony in Three Movements
Prom 42

The *Symphony in Three Movements*, Stravinsky's most dynamic and cogent symphonic work, was written during the Second World War and inspired by his feelings of growing confidence in the inevitable defeat of the Axis powers. A documentary film about scorched-earth tactics in China provided the initial stimulus for the first movement, and the slow movement was originally sketched as possible film music for an adaptation of *The Song of Bernadette* by Stravinsky's fellow Hollywood exile (and Alma Mahler's third husband), Franz Werfel. The finale's fugue was meant to portray the breakdown of the Nazi war machine and the growing power of the Allies.

Dismissed from his post as head of the advanced composition masterclass at the Berlin Academy of Arts in 1933, Schoenberg made his way to France and thence to the USA. But his schemes to mount a fight-back by organising a new Jewish political party in New York were rapidly transformed into a fight to stay alive as he found the climate severely damaging his health. Eventually he had to settle in California, supporting his young family by teaching music to American teenagers for a university that would eventually forcibly retire him on a tiny pension. He set up home in Hollywood, right across the street from the actress Shirley Temple. Budding American film composers flocked to him, hoping to learn 'modernistic' effects, only to recoil rapidly when he proposed teaching them the basic minimum of harmony and counterpoint which he could see they lacked. A few (such as the distinguished Hollywood composer Alfred Newman) stayed to learn from this most remarkable of teachers.

Schoenberg himself never secured a commission for a film score (though he had written an 'imaginary' one in 1930, the *Accompaniment to a Film Scene*). But Hollywood benefited mightily from the flood of European refugees, for whom the film industry offered gainful employment for talents they might otherwise have devoted to opera. In the process, they raised the musical component of the movies to a new importance – none more so than the Austrian-born Erich Wolfgang Korngold, already with a string of operatic hits behind him, who conceived

Béla Bartók (1881–1945)
Concerto for Orchestra
Prom 36
Piano Concerto No. 3
Prom 57

Bartók was in poor health when he composed the *Concerto for Orchestra* (Koussevitzky came to his hospital bedside with the commission) and he probably knew that he was dying while he hurried to finish the Third Piano Concerto as a gift for his second wife. Yet these two works kick-started his posthumous international reputation and were rapidly accepted into the mainstream repertoire. Sometimes said to represent a new 'American-style' Bartók – less dissonant in harmony and more classical in outline than his previous works – they unite an ultimate optimism with tragic, sublimated references to the music of the composer's native Hungary.

Arnold Schoenberg (1874–1951)

Violin Concerto
Prom 40

A Survivor from Warsaw
Prom 67

In his American exile Schoenberg continued to refine and develop his 12-tone technique in eloquent large-scale works such as the Violin Concerto. But he was also beset by continual anxiety about the fate of family and friends left in Europe, and more aware than most of the Nazi threat to the Jewish people, which he had foreseen even in the early 1920s. In *A Survivor from Warsaw* – premiered by largely amateur forces in Albuquerque, New Mexico, in 1948 – he took reports from the Warsaw Ghetto and from Auschwitz and created perhaps the most forceful of all musical commentaries on the Holocaust.

(See also 'Schoenberg', page 50)

the films he scored as operas with speech instead of song and bent his brilliant orchestrational talents to that end. In their different ways, Franz Waxman (German), Max Steiner (Austrian), Miklós Rózsa (Hungarian) and several others followed his lead.

Benjamin Britten arrived in the USA in May 1939, partly at the suggestion of W. H. Auden, not fleeing any overt persecution but because he felt too constricted by English society and hoped to find new stimuli working overseas. When the war came, he found instead that he was cut off. But Britten at least was able to decide to return home, though at significant personal risk. Having braved the sea voyage, he registered as a conscientious objector, and *Peter Grimes* had its triumphant premiere a month after the end of the war.

Bartók was less fortunate. In 1940, fearing the capitulation of his homeland to the Nazis, he left Hungary for the USA, where for three years he wrote almost nothing new; he gave concerts and worked on researching the folk music of Asia Minor. By 1943 funds to support his research had dried up, and he was too ill to accept engagements as a pianist: only fortunate commissions allowed him to produce his last major works.

Bartók had already banned the performance of his music on German and Italian radio, and indignantly demanded to be included in the Nazis' notorious travelling exhibition of 'Degenerate Music' (*Entartete Musik*). When his great contemporary George Enescu heard of this, he exclaimed 'Oh, politics! Bartók's music will still live in the world when these people and their children's children have long been forgotten.'

Enescu himself – his own music partly inspired by that of the gypsies, exiles wherever they might be – remained in his native Romania during the war, and did what he could to help protect Jewish and gypsy musicians from the crypto-Fascist government there. After 1945, when that government was replaced by a crypto-Communist one, he decided he had had enough and went into exile in Paris, a cripple and an old man, to write his last works.

Indeed, the new Communist regimes in Eastern Europe provoked their own post-war wave of exiles – such as György Ligeti, whose exploratory attitudes to the basic elements of music accorded ill with the officially sanctioned aesthetic doctrines of Socialist Realism in his native Hungary.

ABOVE
György Ligeti

LEFT
'Achtung! Stillgestanden!': an SS officer rounds up survivors of the 1943 Warsaw Ghetto uprising

To be alienated from a prevailing ideology and yet unable to escape it creates the condition of the 'internal exile', typified by Karl Amadeus Hartmann in Nazi Germany and, above all, by Shostakovich in Soviet Russia – particularly after 1948, when he and Prokofiev were both officially denounced for pursuing the dictates and dissonances of 'Western formalism'. Such official attitudes were long perpetuated against the rising generation of young Soviet composers – especially since one of the architects of the 1948 denunciations remained the immovable boss of the Composers' Union until its dissolution in 1991. Not only was stylistic experimentation discouraged, but also the expression of religious feeling, particularly strong in an essentially devotional composer like the Estonian Arvo Pärt, who eventually felt constrained to leave the USSR in 1982.

With the fall of Soviet Communism, Pärt's 'internal exile' has come to an end, but paradoxically – like several of the leading figures of his generation from the former Soviet Bloc – he has chosen to remain outside his native country, in Germany, rather than to return to a near-chaotic freedom. Pärt is a striking illustration of the old adage that exile may not be so much a physical fact as a state of mind.

Benjamin Britten (1913–76)

Overture 'Paul Bunyan'

Prom 1

Sinfonia da Requiem

Prom 44

Marooned in the USA by the outbreak of World War II, Britten collaborated with W. H. Auden on *Paul Bunyan*, his first substantial essay in music-theatre, a parable of man in and out of harmony with nature. He also wrote his most important orchestral work so far, the *Sinfonia da Requiem*, expressing his horror of war. Bizarrely, it had been commissioned by the Japanese government in honour of the Imperial family – and was indignantly rejected. By the time it was premiered (in New York in 1941), the USA and Japan had entered the war, the Battle of the Atlantic was at its height, and Britten had taken ship back to the UK.

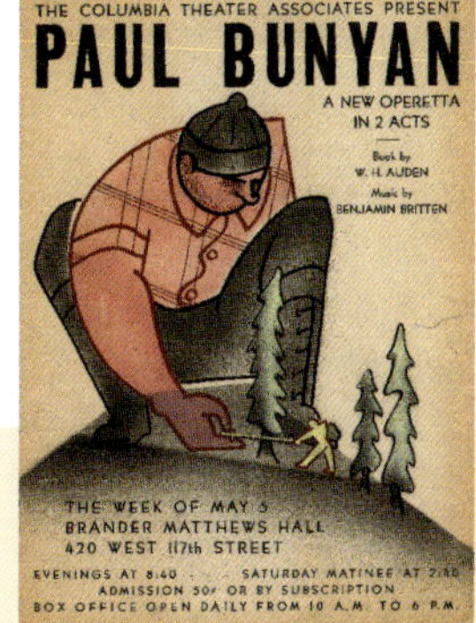

Music of exile at the Proms

Bartók	Concerto for Orchestra	*Prom 36*
	Piano Concerto No. 3	*Prom 57*
Britten	Overture 'Paul Bunyan'	*Prom 1*
	Les illuminations	*Prom 14*
	Sinfonia da Requiem	*Prom 44*
Dvořák	Symphony No. 9, 'From the New World'	*Prom 53*
	'American' Quartet	*PCM 3*
Enescu	Suite No. 1	*Prom 56*
Ligeti	Requiem	*Prom 36*
	Etudes	*PCM 5*
Martinů	Symphony No. 6	*Prom 47*
Pärt	Fratres	*Prom 23*
Prokofiev	Piano Concerto No. 3	*Prom 49*
Rakhmaninov	Rhapsody on a Theme of Paganini	*Prom 42*
	Symphonic Dances	*Prom 57*
Schoenberg	Violin Concerto	*Prom 40*
	A Survivor from Warsaw	*Prom 67*
Stravinsky	Symphony in Three Movements	*Prom 42*
	Suite 'A Soldier's Tale'	*PCM 6*
Verdi	Nabucco: Overture	*Prom 1*
	Aida: Act 1 Prelude and Act 2 (complete)	*Prom 3*
	Nabucco: Chorus of the Hebrew Slaves	*Prom 73*

Gold among the corn

Brendan G. Carroll on Hollywood's musical debt to Europe

Music has been a part of cinema since its earliest days but genuine film music only really developed as an art form in the 1930s, during what is now regarded as Hollywood's golden age. Three factors contributed: the invention of multiple tracking, enabling music to be post-synchronised instead of being recorded live; the rise of Fascism in Europe, bringing a group of highly gifted musicians to Hollywood; and, lastly, the key influence of one man – the Austrian composer Erich Wolfgang Korngold.

Korngold, more than any other composer, brought the language and rhetoric of late 19th- and early 20th-century music to the sound stages of Hollywood. A successful opera composer by the age of 23, he was the first to write film music in long, symphonically developed sequences. He also refined the technique of film scoring to a fine art, introducing the use of the Wagnerian *leitmotif* and creating almost continuous scores, like that for the 1938 Oscar-winner *The Adventures of Robin Hood*, from over 30 different themes for characters and subjects.

Film music came of age with Korngold and his influence was total. Both Max Steiner's *Gone with the Wind* and Miklós Rózsa's *Ben-Hur*, though written in their own composers' distinctive styles, obey Korngoldian practice throughout. In the 1950s Elmer Bernstein (the New York-born son of Austro-Hungarian and Ukrainian parents) created the huge canvas of *The Ten Commandments* in the same manner, while Korngold's influence can still be heard today in such scores as *Star Wars*, *Jurassic Park* and *Braveheart*.

The other émigré composers who fled Europe for the USA defined each film genre. The Hungarian-born Rózsa established the style for *film noir* and historical epics. The German-born Franz Waxman created the horror film score *par excellence* in *The Bride of Frankenstein* before pioneering a true 'American sound' in *The Philadelphia Story* and *A Place in the Sun*, though perhaps his most romantic score (and his own personal favourite) was for Hitchcock's *Rebecca* in 1940. The Ukrainian-born Dimitri Tiomkin almost single-handedly created the 'Western sound' in such classic horse-operas of the Forties and Fifties as *High Noon*, *Red River* and *Rawhide*, though he had taken his stylistic cue from the Vienna-born Steiner's *Dodge City* of 1938.

Sadly, the days when every studio had its own symphony orchestra – and composers of the calibre of Steiner and Korngold creating major scores – are long gone. That this golden age was a direct result of exile and persecution – and that the music written then is now so valued and performed – makes the achievement of these 'exiles in Paradise' all the more remarkable.

The Great Escape
Elmer Bernstein conducts film scores by Korngold, Steiner, Rózsa, Tiomkin and Waxman, as well as by Raksin, Copland, Herrmann and himself
Prom 32 Tuesday 14 August, 7.00pm

Ronald Grant Archive

Lebrecht Collection (Korngold, Waxman) Kobal Collection (Tiomkin, Steiner, Rózsa) Ronald Grant Archive (2001)

2001: A Space Odyssey

It's 33 years since Stanley Kubrick's space-age vision of the mystic origins and evolutionary future of human intelligence first hit our cinema screens. To mark *2001*'s coming-of-age, Proms 2001 offers its own mini-odyssey through some of the movie's most memorable music:

R. Strauss • Also sprach Zarathustra Prom 14
Used to accompany the film's opening titles (and various key astral alignments thereafter), the sunburst opening of Strauss's tone-poem is now synonymous with the mystery of space exploration

György Ligeti • Requiem Prom 36
The choral clusters of Ligeti's 1965 Requiem brilliantly capture the primitive man-apes' awed confusion at the first appearance of the mysterious monolith

J. Strauss II • The Blue Danube Prom 37
Strauss's most famous waltz underscores a weightless ballet for docking spacecraft

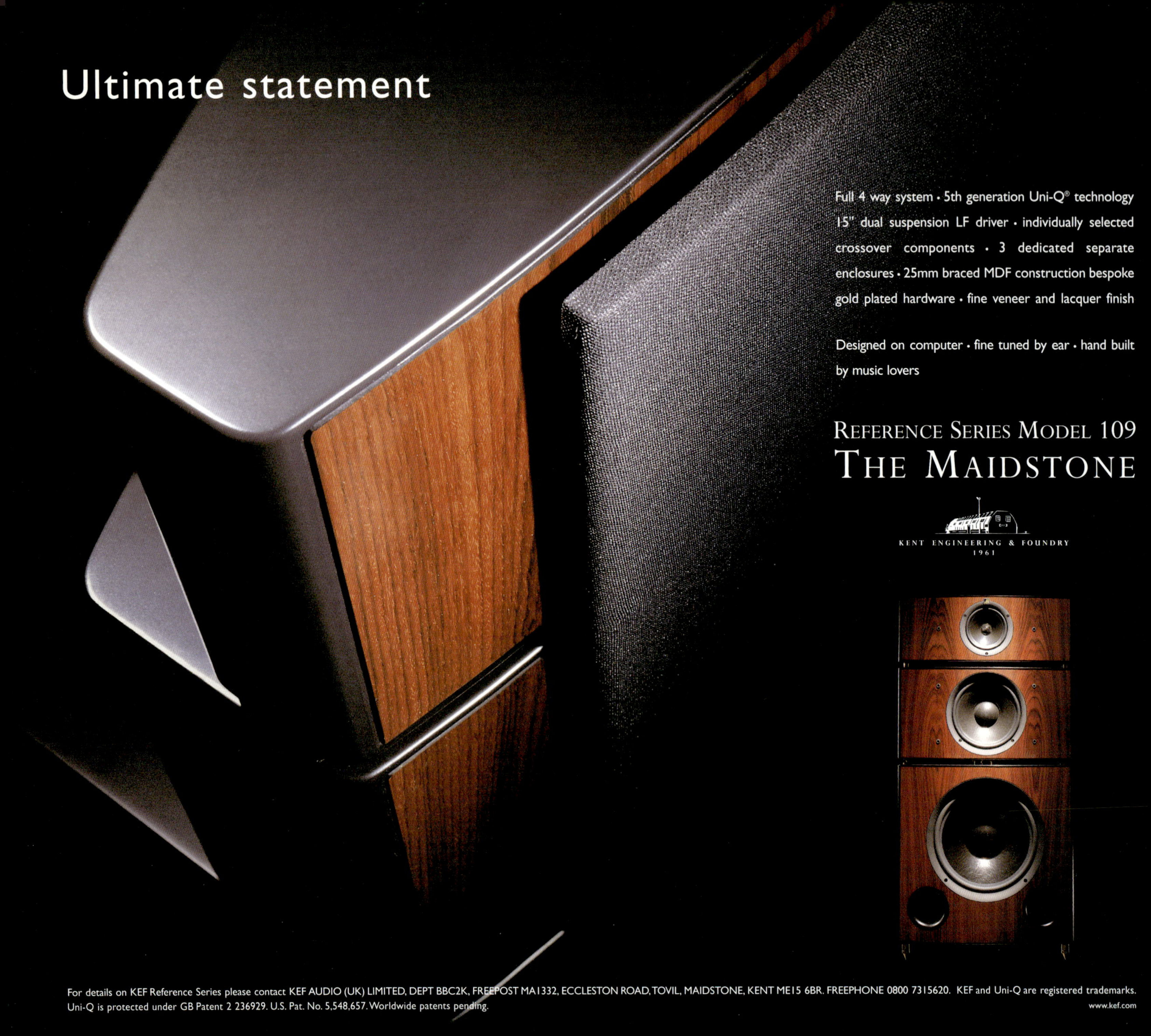

Ultimate statement

Full 4 way system · 5th generation Uni-Q® technology
15" dual suspension LF driver · individually selected
crossover components · 3 dedicated separate
enclosures · 25mm braced MDF construction bespoke
gold plated hardware · fine veneer and lacquer finish

Designed on computer · fine tuned by ear · hand built
by music lovers

REFERENCE SERIES MODEL 109
THE MAIDSTONE

Where can I listen to classical music online?

Got a question?
Just type it in at www.ask.co.uk

From New York City Ballet to theatre from Quebec,

from Wagner's **Die Walküre** to Carles Santos' **Ricardo i Elena**, from Baryshnikov to the Vienna Burgtheater, this year's Festival will leave you spoilt for choice.

Operatic rarities include concert performances of Rossini's **Armida** conducted by Carlo Rizzi, Peter Eötvös' **Three Sisters** and James MacMillan's **Parthenogenesis**, each conducted by its composer, Messiaen's monumental **Saint François d'Assise** conducted by Reinbert de Leeuw, Rameau's **Zoroastre** with Les Arts Florissants and William Christie and Berlioz's **Les Troyens** conducted by Donald Runnicles. And with Mozart's **Idomeneo** conducted by Sir Charles Mackerras, **Così fan tutte** conducted by András Schiff and **Bluebeard's Castle** conducted by Pierre Boulez, along with Scottish Opera's new production of **Die Walküre** and a wonderful new staging of **Die Zauberflöte** from the Aix-en-Provence Festival, the opera programme alone ensures three weeks of fantastic Festival experiences.

And then there's the morning chamber recitals, the highly acclaimed dance programme, international theatre, the world class orchestral concerts . . .

Edinburgh International Festival 12 August – 1 September 2001
For a brochure or for tickets call 0131 473 2000 www.eif.co.uk

it promises to be a colourful festival.

Celebrate these concerts with
the car in front is a
TOYOTA

OUTSTANDING ARTISTS AT THE 2001 PROMS

SIMON RATTLE

MARTHA ARGERICH

DANIEL BARENBOIM

ANTONIO PAPPANO

IAN BOSTRIDGE

BERNARD HAITINK

SARAH CHANG

LEIF OVE ANDSNES

www.emiclassics.com

Green and pleasant lands

From Beethoven to Birtwistle, composers have flocked to
the countryside and ploughed the fields for inspiration.
Piers Burton-Page unearths the rustic roots of pastoral music

PICTURE
Scene by the brook:
Beethoven composes his
Pastoral Symphony (coloured
lithograph from 1834)

'More the expression of feeling than painting.' Those famous words on the handbill for Beethoven's concert in Vienna on 22 December 1808, which began with the first performance of his *Pastoral Symphony*, triggered a subtle shift in the aesthetic landscape of the 19th century. They marked the death-knell of naive musical pictorialism – even if much of this sublime masterpiece is still blatantly naive and descriptive.

What had changed? The *Pastoral Symphony* was not a pioneering work – there was a long tradition of pieces of music, even symphonies, descriptive of rural landscapes peopled with happy shepherds or figures from Antiquity. Why did Beethoven feel the need to be so uncharacteristically defensive?

An answer can be found in Vienna itself. One of its landmarks is the Kahlenberg, a hilly area dotted with vines. Through the woods by the Kahlenberg flows a small stream, easily accessible from Heiligenstadt, one of the places outside the city where Beethoven retreated in summer. In the early 1800s it was an oasis, affording a glimpse of Arcadia. Legend has it that this spot was the inspiration for the 'Scene by the brook' that forms the second movement of the *Pastoral Symphony*.

There is a bust of Beethoven nearby, and the path by the stream is now called the Beethovengang. But grass has been replaced by concrete, smart blocks of flats loom alongside, and Heiligenstadt was long ago swallowed up in the greater Vienna metropolis. It might all

'How happy I am whenever I
can wander in the woods, in
the forests, among the trees,
the rocks! No man could love
the countryside as much as I'
Beethoven, writing in 1808

be a metaphor for the disappearance of a genre that once spoke with a much clearer voice than it does today.

Yet pastoral has always seemed difficult to pin down, and to inhabit unreal terrain. It seems to have something to do with landscapes, and with people. The landscapes of pastoral seem to be remote or isolated, magical or imaginary: an island, or a forest, the Elysian Fields, even the Garden of Eden. Peopling these distant Arcadias are characters faintly incredible: shepherds with seldom a trace of mud on their boots; nymphs and swains who dance to the music of time and aren't worried by the declining rural economy; naughty demigods peeping from behind verdant bushes. If there is a plot of any kind, it usually involves the trials and tribulations of wooing and courtship. Innocence and happiness reign.

The roots of pastoral go right back to Classical Antiquity. Virgil and Ovid, and before them some of the Greeks, used the genre with originality and ingenuity. Even in Antiquity, where the mindset of the average Athenian or Roman was unimaginably different from our own, the same motifs of pastoral innocence and the rural idyll are vividly at (sometimes complex) play – in, for instance, one of the classics of the genre that is regularly held up as a model, the *Idylls* of Theocritus. Narratives of the birth of Christ acquired a strong pastoral tinge, while the Virgin Mary was adored as the fairest flower of the field, a spotless rose.

And then came the Renaissance and its rediscovery of Antiquity and the great pastoral explosion, as poets and painters and composers discovered the pastoral as an ideal vehicle for allegory verging on tactful social commentary. Infinitely adaptable, pastoral is appropriated by many fields. You will find courtly pastoral, political pastoral, Biblical or religious pastoral, pastorals of the self, or of solitude, or of childhood – even (paradoxically) urban pastoral!

Though amorous nightingales nest frequently in the musical landscapes of Couperin and Rameau, the greatest 18th-century expert on nymphs and shepherds, musically speaking, was Handel. German-born, apprenticed in Italy, living in England, he had three separate pastoral traditions at his

TOP LEFT
An indicator board at Vienna's central Landstrasse station signals the next U-bahn service to Heiligenstadt

ABOVE
'And ever against eating cares, lap me in soft Lydian airs': John Milton, poet of *L'Allegro* and *Il Penseroso*, the first two parts of Handel's masque

LEFT
Et in Arcadia ego: can even death disturb the rural idyll of Poussin's shepherds?

RIGHT
'To many a youth, and many a maid, dancing in the chequer'd shade': a scene from Mark Morris's dance version of Handel's *L'Allegro, il Penseroso ed il Moderato*, as revived at English National Opera last year

'While the ploughman near at hand,
Whistles o'er the furrowed land,
And the milkmaid singeth blithe,
And the mower whets his scythe,
And every shepherd tells his tale
Under the hawthorn in the dale,
Straight mine eye hath caught
     new pleasures
Whilst the landscape round
     it measures …'

From John Milton's *L'Allegro*

George Frideric Handel (1685–1759)

L'Allegro, il Penseroso ed il Moderato
Prom 2
Acis and Galatea
Prom 24

Though he had previously written an Italian cantata on the same subject, Handel's *Acis and Galatea*, to a libretto of which John Gay contributed the lion's share, is resolutely English. After *Acis*, Handel wrote no further pastorals until 1732. Then, suddenly, there was an explosion of operas and, in 1740, a late ode: *L'Allegro, il Penseroso ed il Moderato* sets primarily Milton, which is why there are echoes of another strand – the English court masque.

Joseph Haydn (1732–1809)

The Seasons
Prom 26

As he turned 60, Haydn's inventiveness and boldness were at their peak, culminating in the two late oratorios that are masterpieces of identification with their subject. After *The Creation* (1798) came *The Seasons* (1801), one of the first masterpieces of the 19th century. And it has more than a few almost Schubertian touches. Haydn's Arcadia – which in his imagination he saw as the flat fields of his native Burgenland – may be peopled by three rustics, Simon, Hanne and Lucas, who are largely stereotypes, but Haydn seems interested in them as much as in the landscape itself.

Ludwig van Beethoven (1770–1827)

Symphony No. 6, 'Pastoral'

Prom 71

Ralph Vaughan Williams (1872–1958)

Symphony No. 3, 'Pastoral'

Prom 4

Happy peasants, a rippling stream, a brief storm – they are all present in that touchstone of all music in the pastoral mode, Beethoven's *Pastoral Symphony*. But they are not centre-stage. Instead, pastoral meets Romanticism, and in the centre of the landscape is Beethoven himself.

One quality absent from Beethoven's Arcadia – irony – lurks beneath a 20th-century *Pastoral Symphony*, that by Vaughan Williams, inspired by his experiences on the front line in the First World War. And yet Beethoven too seems to sense, and to tell us, that pastoral is not everything, any more.

disposal, each quite different – but hard, these days, to disentangle. Times have gradually changed, of course. Beethoven's nervousness is to do with naivety, the uncomfortable sense that he is toying with unreality. Enter, with the dawn of Romanticism, irony, which allows the continued use of pastoral even as we say we don't believe all those *Tales from the Vienna Woods*, or burbling streams like Smetana's Vltava (in *Má vlast*) and Ives's Housatonic (in *Three Places in New England*), or angelic visions complete with ecstatic sopranos, as in Mahler's Fourth Symphony or *Des Knaben Wunderhorn*. Even Michael Tippett's Rose Lake has been invaded by tourists.

Most composers have been touched by pastoral. Malicious critics claim a whole generation of British composers wrote nothing but 'cowpat' music – among them, anniversarians Rubbra, Finzi and Lambert (*see page 25*). Philip Heseltine, who in his *alter ego* as Peter Warlock wrote many a fine pastoral song, said that Vaughan Williams's *Pastoral Symphony* was 'like a cow looking over a gate'. He was clearly deaf to all its manifold ironies, of war and of fields where only poppies grow. The literary equivalent is A. E. Housman's bitter reinvention of the pastoral mode in *A Shropshire Lad*, which in turn inspired countless song-settings, including many by Butterworth, who was killed by sniper fire in August 1916.

ABOVE

Ralph Vaughan Williams, photographed while on active service in World War I

BELOW

Fields of crosses: the military cemetery at Verdun, c1920

Felix Mendelssohn: portrait by Wilhelm von Schadow (1788–1862), painted in Düsseldorf in 1835

Hector Berlioz: portrait by Gustave Courbet (1819–77)

Titania wakes up beside a bestial Bottom: illustration to *A Midsummer Night's Dream* by Henry Fuseli (1741–1825)

Peter Coleman-Wright as the Narrator – with Babe, the Blue Ox – in the 1997 Royal Opera production of *Paul Bunyan*, Britten's 1941 American operetta

By the dawn of the 20th century, then, pastoral had long since begun to take on new dimensions. Thanks to industrial and political revolutions, and the rise of psychologism, there was an irreversible loss of innocence. Now there are shadows beneath the bucolic surface. Blake had earlier seen the canker in the rose, in a poem given a devastating setting in Britten's *Serenade*. Given his lifelong preoccupation with the 'ceremony of innocence', it is hardly surprising to find Britten often seriously engaged with pastoral. Even his early opera *Paul Bunyan* (about a legendary giant lumberjack) toys with a vision of America tinged with pastoral nostalgia.

More recently, that giant among living British composers, Sir Harrison Birtwistle (whose new BBC commission is premiered in Prom 64), has shown a long-standing interest in exploring the pastoral mode. His stage pieces *Down by the Greenwood Side* (1969) and *Yan Tan Tethera* (1986) – subtitled 'a dramatic pastoral' and 'a mechanical pastoral' respectively – reinvigorated the genre, while his opera *Gawain* (1991) features an Arthurian Green Knight who shares elements with the more folkloric Green Man, as well as a masque of the seasons and several hunting scenes.

If the ironic mode gave pastoral a new lease of life in the 20th century – post-modern pastoral, perhaps – what of the 21st? Though country matters are much in the headlines – fox-hunting, GM crops, foot-and-mouth – there may be a temptation to dismiss pastoral as

Felix Mendelssohn (1809–47)
Incidental music 'A Midsummer Night's Dream'
Prom 53

'The best actors in the world,' announces the Player-King in *Hamlet*, 'tragical, comical, historical, pastoral …' Shakespeare excelled in all these, not just separately but together: the late romances such as *The Tempest* or *The Winter's Tale* are wonderful pastoral amalgams. Elsewhere too, Town and Country (the theme of this year's *Blue Peter* Prom) frequently knock a few edges off each other. *A Midsummer Night's Dream* is a surprisingly edgy entertainment, and if Mendelssohn's magical music is most responsive to its faery element, the rustics – as so often, Shakespeare's truth-tellers – are rather more attractive than the toffs.

Hector Berlioz (1803–69)
Symphonie fantastique
Prom 68

Berlioz, a passionate Virgilian, prefers the personal dramas and the clash of arms in the *Aeneid* to the pastoral pleasures of the *Eclogues*. Only in the Shepherds' Farewell in *L'enfance du Christ* and in the 'Scène aux champs' in the *Symphonie fantastique* does he embrace pastoral – and, even in this last, the rolling timpani seem to foreshadow the witches' ride to come. By contrast, Joseph Canteloube's ever-popular collection of *Songs of the Auvergne* (some of which can be heard on the Last Night) clings to the old images and decks out traditional folk melodies in the genteel orchestral garb of the concert hall.

Benjamin Britten (1913–76)

Spring Symphony
Prom 11

The darker side of pastoral haunts much of the music of Britten, even in the effervescent *Spring Symphony*. It is not just a question of 'strawberries running in the cream', but also of W. H. Auden asking 'What doubtful act allows / Our freedom in this English house / Our picnics in the sun?' It is no surprise to find Britten also absorbed in Mahler (Prom 6) or the anti-illusory poems of Rimbaud (Prom 14) or exploring the underside of night, in the wonderful *Nocturne* (Prom 52). Pastoral innocence is over for good.

Maurice Ravel (1875–1937)

Daphnis and Chloë
Prom 48

The music of Ravel often evokes the distant serenity of Antiquity. *Daphnis and Chloë*, the magical score he wrote for Diaghilev's Ballets Russes, was based on a Greek pastoral romance attributed to one Longus, who flourished in the 3rd century AD. Why the retreat into pastoral classicism, shared incidentally with Debussy's *Prélude à L'après-midi d'un faune* (Prom 47) and Roussel's *Bacchus et Ariane* (Prom 60)? Partly it was a way of making the erotic acceptable. But maybe, too, pastoral offered a relatively neutral backdrop, against which French brilliance of orchestration could be sumptuously foregrounded.

hopelessly outdated. If we are so tempted, we would perhaps do well to heed Theseus's exhortation at the end of *A Midsummer Night's Dream*, when Hippolyta complains that 'This is the silliest stuff that ever I heard'. You're utterly wrong, Theseus says, just use your fancy a little: 'The best in this kind are but shadows, and the worst are no worse, if imagination amend them.' A little imagination may well ensure pastoral's survival, then, and Sally Beamish's new *Knotgrass Elegy*, with its hymn to species under threat from man, may be just the latest echo of a surprisingly long-lived genre.

Pastoral music at the Proms

Beamish	Knotgrass Elegy	*Prom 12*
Beethoven	Symphony No. 6, 'Pastoral'	*Prom 71*
Berlioz	Symphonie fantastique	*Prom 68*
Britten	Overture 'Paul Bunyan'	*Prom 1*
	Spring Symphony	*Prom 11*
	Nocturne	*Prom 52*
	Folk songs	*PCM 2*
Butterworth	Six Songs from 'A Shropshire Lad'	*PCM 2*
Canteloube	Songs of the Auvergne	*Prom 73*
Couperin	Le rossignol en amour	*PCM 1*
Debussy	Prélude à L'après-midi d'un faune	*Prom 47*
Handel	L'Allegro, il Penseroso ed il Moderato	*Prom 2*
	Acis and Galatea	*Prom 24*
Haydn	The Seasons	*Prom 26*
Ives	Three Places in New England	*Prom 30*
Mendelssohn	Incidental music 'A Midsummer Night's Dream'	*Prom 53*
Montéclair	Pan et Syrinx	*PCM 1*
Rameau	Rossignols amoureux	*PCM 1*
Ravel	Daphnis and Chloë	*Prom 48*
Rodrigo	Concierto pastoral	*Prom 37*
Roussel	Bacchus et Ariane	*Prom 60*
Schubert	The Shepherd on the Rock	*PCM 8*
Smetana	Vltava	*Prom 37*
J. Strauss II	The Blue Danube	*Prom 37*
Takemitsu	Garden Rain	*Prom 64*
Tippett	The Rose Lake	*Prom 71*
Vaughan Williams	Symphony No. 3, 'Pastoral'	*Prom 4*

ABOVE
Vaslav Nijinsky as the amorous Faun in his 1912 staging of Debussy's *Prélude à L'après-midi d'un faune* for Diaghilev's Ballets Russes

LEFT
Daphnis and Chloë by François Pascal Gérard (1770–1837)

Fields of vision

Finzi, Rubbra, Lambert and Vaughan Williams:
Roderic Dunnett looks back at four 20th-century
composers who helped shape Britain's musical landscape

BELOW
'Shady Quiet'
by Samuel Palmer (1805–81)

Conjure up English 'Pastoral' and one thinks, perhaps, first and foremost not of music, but of art or literature: of Constable, Palmer and Cotman; or that strand of writing which links Spenser and Shakespeare, Wordsworth, John Clare and Richard Jefferies, and the 20th-century sensibilities of Edward Thomas or Laurie Lee.

Yet, when applied to 20th-century English music, the term 'pastoral' tends all too readily to be used with a sneer. Arguably, it was rival musicians who had most to gain from such inaccurate slurs. It was Elisabeth Lutyens, that early English serialist, who allegedly coined the phrase 'the cowpat school' to describe her more bucolically inclined contemporaries. As for Philip Heseltine

– alias Peter Warlock – his infamous comparison of Vaughan Williams's *Pastoral Symphony* to 'a cow looking over a gate' reveals the Ezra Pound of English music as a not wholly disinterested cynic with a musical agenda of his own. For Warlock was something of a ruralist himself, and shared a rumbustious household (just one village up from Samuel Palmer's Shoreham) with the most engagingly pastoral of all the 1920s generation, Ernest – jolly 'Jack' – Moeran; whereas Vaughan Williams's symphony was, as we now know, an eloquent war elegy, begun in 1916, when the composer had a medic's-eye view of the horrors of the Somme. The cow-and-gate comment thus tells us more about Warlock's wit,

with its Boulezian rapier-thrusts, its crisp venom worthy of Debussy's *nom de guerre* Monsieur Croche, than about Vaughan Williams's work itself.

Another good friend of the saturnine Warlock was the highly un-pastoral, Satie-influenced Constant Lambert. It was Warlock's grisly suicide (by gas-poisoning) in 1930 that inspired Lambert's bleakly pessimistic Piano Concerto of 1931 – Lambert himself called it a 'musical St Vitus's dance'. But in 1924, while still a student, the 19-year-old Lambert had begun another piano concerto, conceived – in more Impressionistic style – for piano, trumpets, timpani and strings; and there's a rare chance to hear this four-movement work – recently reconstructed from the composer's surviving two-piano sketch – in the Britten Sinfonia's

Late-Night Prom (Prom 52).

Lambert's choral extravaganza *The Rio Grande*, premiered on BBC radio in 1928 (and a highlight of this year's Last Night), could not be further away: fields again, but here the cotton-picking fields of the deep American South, frame its visionary, jazz-inspired evocation of an imaginary Central American vista. Lambert, who was music director of the Vic-Wells (later Sadler's Wells) Ballet from 1931 until his death 50 years ago, was as much a master of syncopated habanera, tango and wistful blues as he was of the Stravinskyan punchiness peppering his scintillating youthful ballet scores, *Romeo and Juliet* (staged by Diaghilev in 1926) and *Pomona* (1927). The idea for *Prize Fight* (Prom 52) – a swashbuckling 1924 depiction of a Joe Louis-style tussle between a black

and a white boxer – came from Vaughan Williams, who was plotting a boxing-match scene for his own 'pastoral' opera *Hugh the Drover*.

One composer who did actually compose a *Pastoral* was the uncowpattish Arthur Bliss, whose 1929 work (subtitled *Lie Strewn the White Flocks*) comprises a charming anthology evoking a Theocritean landscape. Bliss – a wartime director of music for the BBC, distinguished Master of the Queen's Music, and a composer celebrated for explosive avant-garde works, motoric film scores (notably *Things to Come*) and electrifying ballets (*Checkmate, Miracle in the Gorbals* and *Adam Zero*, all premiered by Lambert) – was friend and adviser to, among many others, two composers 10 years his junior: Edmund Rubbra and Gerald Finzi.

Finzi (born on 14 July 1901) is one whose comparatively slender output has held its own since his premature death in 1956. The Clarinet Concerto, *Dies natalis, Intimations of Immortality* and several song-cycles pay tribute to Finzi's gift for long-lined melody and refined word-setting. *Farewell to Arms* (Prom 52 again) is an enchanting treatment of two lesser-known 16th- and 17th-century poets, George Peele and Ralph Knevet, who both evoke the image of a warrior's helmet being turned into a beehive. A work in which Finzi's 'Bachian' idiom comes close to *Dies natalis, Farewell to Arms* was first heard in a BBC broadcast in April 1945, sung by Eric Greene, with the BBC Northern Orchestra conducted by Charles Groves.

Finzi's *Let Us Garlands Bring*, one of the works in Thomas Allen's Proms Chamber Music recital (PCM 2), is a set of five Shakespeare songs, dedicated to Vaughan Williams on his 70th birthday; the earliest, 'Fear no more the heat o' the Sun' (the brothers' lament for Imogen, from *Cymbeline*), ranks among the most moving of all 20th-century plaints – an evocative echo of the Elizabethan and Jacobean lute-song ethos of Campion and Dowland. *The Fall of the Leaf* (another Last Night novelty) was originally destined to be a movement in an abandoned Chamber Symphony; it was Bliss who urged Finzi to recycle it as a separate piece. The slightly more Elgarian *Romance* (also Prom 52) was likewise intended for a planned Serenade; it remained unheard in public until 1951. That same year Finzi began what was to become his last major work, the Cello Concerto (Prom 11); first heard in 1955, at the 10th Cheltenham Festival, it was brought to the Proms in August 1956, less than a month before Finzi died. It's a scorcher of a work: brusque, vigorous, stormy, challenging, and with a slow movement – by turns lulling (though scarcely 'pastoral') and rending – that brought tears to the eyes of John Barbirolli, who had conducted its first performance and later revived it at the Proms.

Finzi dedicated another work, his *Milton Sonnets*, to his close friend and colleague Edmund Rubbra. Born the

same year (23 May 1901), Rubbra shared Finzi's acute sensibility in word-setting (Spenser, the doyen of Virgil-inspired Elizabethan 'pastoralists', was a favourite), but devoted his main energies to a series of major, and distinctly un-pastoral, symphonic and chamber works. If Finzi's Cello Concerto has echoes of 18th-century *Sturm und Drang*, Rubbra's wartime Fourth Symphony (Prom 9) is, from its awesome, astringent, oppressive

opening, a massive outpouring of static energy and electrifying intensity. Rubbra not only dedicated this symphony to Henry Wood, but conducted its 1942 Proms premiere himself, in battle dress. British taste preferred the tuneful Fifth, however, which partly justifies *Times* music critic Frank Howes's outwardly curious claim that Rubbra's works 'declare their basic allegiance to what may be called the English pastoral style'. Yet Howes rightly pointed out that a

ABOVE
Gerald Finzi

RIGHT
Edmund Rubbra pictured in 1949 with his first wife Antoinette at Valley Cottage, near Speen in the Chilterns, where they had settled in the early 1930s

'Rubbra's Fourth Symphony shows ... that originality consists, not in the conscious forging of a new idiom, but in the personal handling of a common tongue'
J. A. Westrup, *Musical Times*, July 1942

true understanding of 'pastoral' implies not Heseltine's contemplating quadrupeds but the self-abandoned vitality of Gay's *The Beggar's Opera*, of the madrigal and the round, and of a tradition of folk song that was as much earthy, full-throated and rollicking – like one of Warlock and Moeran's evenings in The Five Bells at Eynsford – as mooching. Not just silent dawns, ruddy sunsets and homeward-plodding ploughmen, but pub-opening time too.

If any symphony hovers close to the generally received idea of 'pastoral', it is – paradoxically – Vaughan Williams's *A London Symphony* (Prom 13). No British symphony of the pre-war period conjures up such serenity as that slow arc of a tune in the second movement. Much else is bluster and noise, London cries, and the blare and honk of traffic, as vital and imaginative as equivalent works by Debussy, Ives and even Gershwin. The same composer's *A Sea*

Symphony (Prom 67) is a magnificent, ebullient, evocative setting of verses by Walt Whitman, for which Vaughan Williams conjures up a Turner-esque wash of stormy colours. His *Serenade to Music* (Prom 1) is a setting of words from the start of Act 5 of Shakespeare's *The Merchant of Venice* ('How sweet the moonlight sleeps upon this bank'); composed for Henry Wood's golden jubilee concert at the Royal Albert Hall on 5 October 1938, it offers a rapturous invocation, a transfiguration of sweet sounds, that washes over you and simply sweeps you away. Like 'Silent Noon' (PCM 2), one of the songs from RVW's achingly beautiful early Rossetti cycle *The House of Life*, I could happily listen to it until the cows come home.

Finzi at the Proms

Prom 11	Cello Concerto
Prom 52	Farewell to Arms; Romance
Prom 73	The Fall of the Leaf
PCM 2	Let Us Garlands Bring

Lambert at the Proms

Prom 52	Prize Fight; Piano Concerto (1924)
Prom 73	The Rio Grande

Rubbra at the Proms

Prom 9	Symphony No. 4

Vaughan Williams at the Proms

Prom 1	Serenade to Music
Prom 4	Symphony No. 3, 'Pastoral'
Prom 13	A London Symphony
Prom 67	A Sea Symphony
PCM 2	Silent Noon

OXFORD
UNIVERSITY PRESS

... music now

2001 richard causton 30
2002 gerald barry 50
john buller 75

... and then

2002 william walton 100

oxford university press
repertoire promotion department
70 baker street
london w1u 7dn
tel: +44 (0)20 7616 5900
fax: +44 (0)20 7616 5901
e-mail: repertoire.promotion@oup.co.uk
website: www.oup.co.uk/music/repprom

If music
be
the food of *love*...

...*Feast yourselves*

With Systemline, you can enjoy your favourite music whenever & wherever you desire. Hi-Fi sound

and vision in any room and it all happens with the touch of a single button. What could be simpler?

....Love life ....Love music ....Love Systemline

Wherever you may be

Multi-Room Sound & Vision **Systemline**
S4

(A colour brochure featuring the full product range is available on request)

UPLIFTING THOUGHTS
Nº 15

Henderson Global Investors wins
160 investment awards in six years

Thoughts that count
For more information: quote ref BD 46
0500 707 707
www.henderson.com

Henderson
Global Investors

An AMP Company

Source: Henderson Global Investors based on 1st, 2nd and 3rd place awards/commendations since 1995. Please remember that past performance is not necessarily a guide to future performance. The value of an investment and the income from it can fall as well as rise as a result of market and currency fluctuations and you may not get back the amount originally invested. Tax assumptions may change if the law changes and the value of tax relief will depend upon individual circumstances. Henderson Global Investors is the name under which Henderson Global Investors Limited and Henderson Investment Funds Limited (both regulated by IMRO and the Personal Investment Authority), Henderson Fund Management plc and Henderson Administration Limited (both regulated by IMRO) provide investment products and services. 4 Broadgate, London EC2M 2DA.

BBC SINGERS

Chief Conductor: Stephen Cleobury

2001 FESTIVAL APPEARANCES IN SALZBURG, STRASBOURG, ALDEBURGH, EDINBURGH, CHELTENHAM, DEAL, SPITALFIELDS & AT THE BBC PROMS

"A highly successful, imaginative and superbly sung collection."
(Illuminare: Carols for a New Millennium)

Ivan Moody, International Record Review

"The elite BBC Singers."

Fiona Hook, Evening Standard

"The BBC Singers sallied superbly through Schnittke's Concerto for Mixed Choir."

Geoff Brown, The Times

JAMES BRABAZON

For more information about forthcoming concerts, join the BBC Singers free mailing list
Tel: 020 7765 1862
Email: singers@bbc.co.uk
www.bbc.co.uk/singers

Living with the best quality sound and video can be a compromise.

At Meridian we have ways of solving the problem. The Meridian digital audio system is intelligent.

This helps provide the finest sound without you changing the furniture. Meridian digital surround sound systems have been designed from the start to provide the best music *and* a great home theatre.

All our products from CD/DVD players to the latest in digital loudspeakers work as a matched system controlled from one handset so you can have the best of both worlds – performance without compromise.

BOOTHROYD STUART

MERIDI∆N©

Meridian Audio Limited
Stonehill, Stukeley Meadows,
Huntingdon, PE29 6EX
Tel (0) 1480 52144
Fax (0) 1480 432948

http://www.meridian-audio.com

'It is, as Adams's music has been before, jazzy and melancholy. But, a heavier ship, its take-offs are more gravity-defying; its melodies more winsome; its colours more dazzling; its jazz jazzier; its melancholy more devastating … Everything is bigger and better'
Mark Swed on the premiere of
Adams's Naive and Sentimental Music
(LA Times, 22 February 1999)

John Adams (born 1947)

Michael Steinberg charts 20 years in the life of a composer who long since outgrew his 'minimalist' tag

How nice that the first of John Adams's works to be heard at this year's Proms (and on the First Night too) should be *Harmonium* – the work that first put Adams on the musical map in his own country.

Harmonium sets poetry by John Donne and Emily Dickinson, and was introduced in April 1981 in San Francisco, the part of the world where Adams has lived for 30 years. The excitement before those San Francisco Symphony concerts was all about the belated first appearance in the Bay Area of a renowned soloist (and there was the additional fillip of the leader's violin being stolen under rather piquant circumstances that afternoon), but what everyone who was there that week remembers about those concerts is the delightful shock of *Harmonium*, with its fascinating treatment of the text, sometimes used as if it were part of the instrumental fabric, but so compelling, vivid and illuminating as musical poetry. And, above all, there was the torrential energy of this new work.

Adams is a New Englander: his full name, John Coolidge Adams, is a New England cliché. He learnt much about music from his father, with whom he studied the clarinet, while Walter Piston,

the ultimate New Englander among American composers and a country neighbour, was a kindly mentor. At Harvard, his principal teacher was Leon Kirchner, who had emerged from the exacting schooling of Schoenberg, Bloch and Sessions. Everything was set for Adams to study in Europe for a bit and then to settle into a nice East Coast academic position.

Expect the unexpected. His father gave him John Cage's *Silence* as a graduation present. That book may not in itself have been enough to turn Adams's life around, but it was a reminder that there was more, much more, to the world than he had yet experienced. In any event, he loaded his possessions into a Volkswagen, drove to California, found a job as a fork-lift operator, and became part of the Bay Area's lively music scene, absorbing jazz, electronics and the work of such living American composers as Cage, Morton Feldman, Terry Riley and Robert Ashley. Soon he was teaching and conducting at the San Francisco Conservatory, and then Edo de Waart, his first steadfast supporter among important conductors, took him on as the San Francisco Symphony's new-music adviser and eventually

composer-in-residence. By the mid-1980s, Adams was making his living entirely as a composer and conductor.

He had also fallen in love with consonance and with pulse. (How un-Harvard could you get?) His best works from the 1970s – *Shaker Loops* and *Common Tones in Simple Time* – glow with the excitement of discovery, unlike the scores, stale and matt, of most of the born-again 'neo-tonalists'. Adams seemed to be aligned with the minimalists, but even before that first performance of *Harmonium*, he was already describing himself as a minimalist who was bored with minimalism. Adams is a man of immense inquisitiveness and with a wide-ranging appetite for a rich, varied, interesting and nourishing artistic diet. Even from the beginning, his tones were not that common nor his time so simple, and, without forsaking his early love, he has sought – and found – an ever-broader harmonic and rhythmic language, always in the cause of bigger expressive needs.

Harmonium was predictive of two factors that were to determine Adams's development. One was the love of beautiful and evocative words, a love that would lead him to Alice Goodman's fine opera librettos, *Nixon in China* and *The Death of Klinghoffer*; to his tender and touching Walt Whitman solo cantata for baritone, *The Wound-Dresser*; and to his most beautiful achievement so far, the radiant *El niño*, a staged nativity oratorio introduced last Christmas in Paris, and many of whose

LEFT
John Adams at Tilden Park, Berkeley, California, in May 1995

texts are by Hispanic women poets. An essential collaborator in the formation of all these projects has been Peter Sellars, the director (and so much more).

The other factor was Adams's discovery that he was by nature a 'big' composer, one with capacious lungs. He has written short pieces that have served conductors, audiences, his publisher and his own bank account well: *The Chairman Dances*, a kind of out-take from *Nixon in China*, is the best-known example; *Short Ride in a Fast Machine* – originally written in 1986 as a fanfare for the opening of a festival in Massachusetts (and due to be played at this year's Last Night of the Proms) – is another. Yet a couple of years after *Harmonium*, Adams took the risk of writing a very long piece – a risk, because received wisdom had it that conductors only dared to programme new pieces if they were fanfare-length. But *Harmonielehre*, named after Schoenberg's extraordinary treatise on harmony (and beyond) – Adams has always liked referential titles – runs for 40 minutes or so. Conductors grabbed it up, and they still do, and audiences love this not-at-all-short ride on a complex machine whose middle movement, 'The Anfortas Wound', brings some of the most intensely expressive music written in the 20th century's second half.

The two operas are probing, wise and beautiful. They have also angered some people by maintaining, in the case of *Nixon in China*, that the Nixons,

Chou En-lai and Mao Tse-tung are intricate human beings deserving, among other things, of our compassion (only Dr Kissinger is treated without mercy) and, in the case of *The Death of Klinghoffer*, that in the everlasting miseries of the Middle East virtue is not confined to one side only.

Among Adams's instrumental works, the Violin Concerto has become a repertory piece, with performances now reaching into triple figures and interpreters including such luminaries as Gidon Kremer, Vadim Repin and Leila Josefowicz. In *Century Rolls*, a piano concerto recently written for Emanuel Ax, Adams offers to take on the Ravel Concerto in G and Stravinsky's *Capriccio*; in *Gnarly Buttons* (heard at the 1998 Proms), he has given clarinettists the gift of a new virtuoso concerto for his own instrument; while in *Naive and Sentimental Music* – a title taken from Schiller's famous essay on art – he has written an eloquent score even more generous in scale than *Harmonielehre*: Adams himself will

conduct the work's London premiere in Prom 62. On the drawing-board now are a solo work for the pianist Garrick Ohlsson (who hopes it will be a big piece) and a new orchestral work that will have its first London hearing when the composer himself conducts it at the Barbican next year.

Each of Adams's key works over the past 20 years since that memorable *Harmonium* premiere – and I am thinking particularly of *Harmonielehre*, *Nixon in China*, the Violin Concerto and *El niño* – has been not just a splendid achievement in its own right but has opened a door on to a world of new exploration and development. To be part of this journey, even as a witness, is an exciting privilege for us all.

John Adams at the Proms

Prom 1   Harmonium
Prom 62 Naive and Sentimental Music;
         Le livre de Baudelaire (Debussy,
         arr. Adams)
Prom 73 Short Ride in a Fast Machine

LEFT
President Nixon's arrival at Peking Airport: the opening scene from John Adams's opera *Nixon in China*, as given at English National Opera last year in a revival of Peter Sellars's original 1987 staging

Bill Rafferty/ENO

Commuters generally keep themselves to themselves. However it seems that the levels of income and capital growth offered by ABN AMRO Fund Managers' range of unit trusts, is prompting conversation in the most unlikely of places. With our international resources and award winning investment team the word is spreading rapidly, so listen out - it's worth hearing.

PROMS

Stowe School

Please Contact:
The Registrar
Stowe School
Buckingham
MK18 5EH
Tel: 01280 818000
Fax: 01280 818181

Set in Buckinghamshire (35 miles from Oxford, 55 miles from London)
A Stowe education teaches people to think deeply, to think about others and to think for themselves.
Boarding School with boys from 13-18 and Girls 16-18 (HMC)
580 pupils (540 Full Boarders)

YAN PASCAL TORTELIER WITH THE BBC Philharmonic

CHANDOS ARTISTS
AT THE 2001 PROMS

RICHARD HICKOX WITH THE BBC National Orchestra of Wales

Chandos Records Ltd, Chandos House, Commerce Way, Colchester, Essex CO2 8HQ, UK   Tel: +44 (0) 1206 225225   E-mail: enquiries@chandos.net   Website: www.chandos.net

Royal Philharmonic Orchestra

DANIELE GATTI AND THE ROYAL PHILHARMONIC ORCHESTRA
ONE OF THE MOST EXCITING MUSICAL PARTNERSHIPS IN THE WORLD TODAY

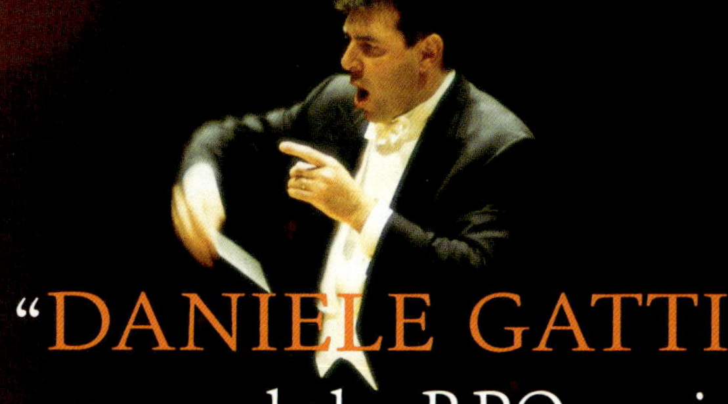

"DANIELE GATTI
has turned the RPO . . . into
a FORCE TO BE RECKONED WITH. Their Prom
[1 August 2000] found them on BLISTERING FORM . . .
A RIVETING EVENING . . . The rich, sensual RPO
sound and Gatti's fondness for EXTREME DYNAMICS
and tempi are telling in this music" THE GUARDIAN

For more information about the Royal Philharmonic Orchestra's concerts with Daniele Gatti,
call for a free brochure 020 7608 2381 or visit our website www.rpo.co.uk

Giuseppe Verdi (1813–1901)

Andrew Porter hails the centenary of the best loved and most humane of opera composers

ABOVE

Title-page of the libretto for *Nabucco*, Verdi's third opera and first international success. The Act 3 'Chorus of the Hebrew Slaves' ('Va, pensiero') became Verdi's most famous piece and was sung by the crowds at his funeral procession in 1901

LEFT

Portrait of Giuseppe Verdi in 1886 by Giovanni Boldini

Pianse ed amò per tutti! – 'He wept and loved for all!' In a 1901 ode *On the Death of Giuseppe Verdi* the poet Gabriele d'Annunzio essayed a five-word summary of what a great composer had meant not just to his countrymen but to the world. And perhaps we can add a third verb, 'laughed'. Verdi's last opera, *Falstaff* – that miracle of grace and musical refinement produced at La Scala, Milan, in 1893, when Verdi was already in his 80th year – brought an old man's acceptance that the world had changed around him. It's a happy, high-spirited work, and also a 'statement' triumphantly proclaiming – after several seasons when Wagner's *Lohengrin*, *Die Meistersinger* and *Tannhäuser* had been big on the bills of Italy's leading theatre – Verdi's own musical and moral ideals.

It was a dark world-picture that he had painted before, one in which 'the force of destiny' thwarts every decent impulse and denies any hope of happiness. There are no happy endings in his earlier operas, except for the comedy *Un giorno di regno* (1840) and, up to a point, *Stiffelio* (1850). There had been two recurrent themes. One was troubled father-daughter relationships, explored in 18 of the 28 works (and in the oft-contemplated, never-completed *King Lear*). The other? That honour and duty drive an upright man to choices that conflict with his hopes of personal happiness.

By the standards of the day, Verdi was a late starter, already 26 when his first (and first father-daughter) drama, *Oberto*, had its Scala premiere, in 1839. *Oberto* had a run of 14 performances, and was brought back for 17 more the following year when *Un giorno di regno* flopped. In 1842 Verdi hit the jackpot with *Nabucco*, which had a run of 65 performances during the year, a figure unequalled in the Scala annals before or since! 'Va, pensiero' (the 'Chorus of the Hebrew Slaves') is the first of his stirring patriotic choruses; others followed in *I lombardi* (1842), *Ernani* (1843) and *Macbeth* (1847).

With *Nabucco*, Verdi entered what he later called his 'years in the galleys', turning out, churning out, two or three operas a year. Most of them were played worldwide. In those days, opera audiences were eager to hear, and singers were eager to sing, new operas; and Verdi – as before him Rossini (until his early retirement) and then Donizetti (until madness checked the splendid outpouring of his last active years) had done – met that demand. Then the pace slowed. Financially secure, and with *Rigoletto* (1851), *Il trovatore* and *La traviata* (both 1853) established in the international repertory, he withdrew from the hurly-burly of Italian operatic life. After *Un ballo in maschera* – composed for but rejected by Naples, and diluted by Italian censorship before its Rome premiere in 1859 – Verdi accepted only (well-paid) foreign commissions: *La forza del destino* for St Petersburg (1862), *Don Carlos* for the Paris Opéra (1867), *Aida* for Cairo (1871). He wanted to work on his own uncompromising terms, to his vision of what serious opera should be. Finally, after years of silence, there were *Otello* (1887) and *Falstaff* (1893), composed,

Antonio Pappano conducts Verdi's *Four Sacred Pieces* in Prom 44

'Verdi always said that he was a *contadino*, a man born from farmer stock, and the earth was always important for him – birth and rebirth in nature. In that sense his religion was pantheistic. As to whether his religious music sounds more operatic than religious: in Italian religion the fear of God is so great that the imagination runs wild thinking of every conceivable punishment which the sinner faces. That lends itself to dramatic treatment, but it doesn't mean that this is operatic music with a religious text.'

Mark Elder conducts an all-Verdi programme in Prom 3

'I thought it would be exciting to devise a programme that showed the range of Verdi's operas. We begin with the overture to *Nabucco*, his first great success. It's a visceral piece, crude in many ways, but its raw energy is characteristic of Verdi's personality.

Then we move to the first act of *Il trovatore*, in which the vocal style has its roots in the past, in the world of Donizetti and Mercadante. But *Trovatore* has a special quality of inspiration to it; one feels it was written at white heat. Yes, it's difficult to sing, but it's not just about tunes and effects, it's about Verdi's ability to create a sense of dramatic space over a 30-minute stretch.

For contrast, that's followed by the first scene of Act 4 of *Don Carlos* – Verdi at his most private, intimate and grief-laden. Up to this point in the opera, we've been watching kings, princes and princesses in their public roles, behaving as they must in the rigorously controlled world of the 16th-century Spanish court. But here we see how lonely and unhappy they are behind that façade, while the orchestra takes on the role of character-moulding, commenting on and supporting every flicker of emotion in the dialogues.

After the interval, we do the whole of Act 2 of *Aida*, with its Triumphal March and gloriously public finale. But we preface it with the beautiful prelude that opens the opera – a little symphonic poem which summarises everything that follows.

What is so remarkable about Verdi is the way he sought out literary sources which provided just the kind of dramatic situations that his music could ignite.'

he said, for his private satisfaction.

And yet – there's nearly always an 'and yet' when one tries to define a great composer's aspirations – Verdi also declared more than once that the clink of the box-office till was the surest measure of an opera's success. When an ambitious new opera failed to catch on, he tried to meet public criticism without compromising his own vision. So *Stiffelio* became *Aroldo*; the sprawling *Forza* was reshaped; the long, unwieldy *Don Carlos*, already much cut before its premiere, was further abridged and tightened.

In his quest for subjects, Verdi sought unconventional characters and plights, expressed in unconventional verse forms ('the odder the better') that would suggest new kinds of musical treatment. A murderous king and queen racked by remorse; a hunchback as hero; a contemporary prostitute as heroine … There had been precedents in Rossini and Donizetti for such things as Macbeth's dagger soliloquy and Rigoletto's 'Pari siamo', the 'dialectical' duets of *Stiffelio*, *Luisa Miller* and *La traviata*; the long, linked sequences of *Il trovatore*. Back in 1851, Verdi told the *Trovatore* librettist, Cammarano, that he wished operas could be 'continuous', not made up of separate numbers. In the study scene of *Don Carlos* (Act 4 scene 1), the king's long aria, the interview with the Grand Inquisitor, the confrontation with the queen that becomes a quartet, the Elizabeth-Eboli exchange (which flowered into a duet, dropped before the first night), and Eboli's final aria proceed in one long dramatic sweep.

Sometimes Verdi 'retrenched'. After the mixed reception of the first version of *Simon Boccanegra* (1857) – a confusing drama that spans three generations and 25 years – he turned to a tight, sure-fire libretto that Scribe had written, long before, for the French composer Auber, and the result, *Un ballo in maschera*, is one of Verdi's surprisingly few mature operas that – apart from the censorship troubles – needed no revision. (Even *Otello* and *Falstaff* have alternative episodes.)

After *Forza* and *Don Carlos* had been found unwieldy, Verdi welcomed in *Aida* a drama that he called distinctly conventional, but well shaped. *Aida* combines intense personal encounters with high spectacle. When it reached the Opéra in 1880, Verdi won at last the decisive Paris success that had so long eluded him.

All his life, the anti-clerical Verdi composed religious music – music to be sung in the Temple of Solomon at Jerusalem, a Protestant preaching-house, a Spanish convent and two Spanish monasteries, the Temple of Vulcan beside the Nile, rebuilt in representation on the opera stage. The *Requiem* – 'religious'

ABOVE
Giuseppe Verdi, photographed in 1899

ABOVE
Aida: costume design for
the Cairo premiere

RIGHT
Verdi and the Censor:
a caricature by
Melchiorre Delfico

music for concert performance,
honouring the writer Alessandro
Manzoni – appeared three years after
Aida. It incorporated an earlier 'Libera
me' composed for a collaborative
Requiem intended to honour Rossini,
and a 'Lacrimosa' based on a Philip-
Carlos duet dropped from *Don Carlos*.
The great work is at once a monument
to Italian genius as Verdi perceived it
in Rossini and Manzoni; a blazing
affirmation of his belief in an Italian
music where the orchestra is very
important but the vocal lines are
paramount; and the climax of all those
scenes, some tender, some terrifying, in
which he had sought to express his vision
of suffering, suppliant humanity.

The *Four Sacred Pieces* come as a
coda. The *Ave Maria* (1888–9) is little
more than a puzzle serenely solved. The
Laudi alla Vergine Maria (also 1888–9)

is like a tender sequel to Desdemona's
prayer in *Otello*. But the two post-
Falstaff works – the *Stabat Mater* and
Te Deum (1895–7) – are important.
The *Stabat Mater* packs into a small
space elements of a Passion (both
narrative and meditation), a 'Dies irae',
a 'Libera me' and an 'In paradisum'. The
double-choir *Te Deum* is harmonically
adventurous and very dramatic. Several
letters attest to the value Verdi placed on
these works. They form an unexpected
but ardent *opus ultimum*.

Prom 3	Nabucco, overture; Il trovatore, Act 1 scene 2; Don Carlos, Act 4 scene 1; Aida, Act 1 prelude and Act 2 (complete)
Prom 44	Four Sacred Pieces
Prom 72	Requiem
Prom 73	La forza del destino, overture; Nabucco, Chorus of the Hebrew Slaves

**Daniele Gatti conducts
Verdi's *Requiem* in
Prom 72**

'You read that Verdi was not a religious
person, but for me the greatest art always
has a sense of the religious. He wrote his
Requiem in memory of Manzoni, but I
consider it a work dedicated to God. Last
year I conducted it in Tel Aviv during Easter
Week, and in that country, at this political
moment, I have to say, as a Catholic, that
it was a privilege to perform it.'
Conductor interviews by Nick Kimberley

Joaquín Rodrigo (1901–99)

Martin Anderson celebrates the centenary of a Spanish composer who wrote three of the most famous notes in 20th-century music

Whistle the opening three notes of the main theme to the slow movement of Rodrigo's *Concierto de Aranjuez* and the chances are that almost anyone else will be able to pick up the tune and continue it. Not many composers penetrate the popular imagination so profoundly: Beethoven managed it with the opening of the Fifth Symphony and the 'Joy' theme of the Ninth, but in both cases it took him a note more than Rodrigo required.

It has proved a Pyrrhic success. The *Concierto de Aranjuez* has almost entirely overshadowed the rest of Rodrigo's prodigious output, which totals over 170 works for a striking variety of forces, from full orchestra and chorus, via ballets, oratorio and film music, to solo pieces for all sorts of instruments, including piano, cello, accordion, harmonica – and, of course, guitar. It would be an astonishing achievement for any composer, let alone one who lost his eyesight at the age of 3. And he didn't stop composing until 1987, writing his music in braille and then dictating it to a copyist.

Rodrigo was born in Sagunto, Valencia, on 22 November 1901, the name-day of St Cecilia, patron saint of music (12 years later Benjamin Britten had the same auspicious birthday). The near-total loss of his sight in a diphtheria epidemic had an upside: it allowed his natural musicality to develop without the conventional distractions of childhood. His parents hired a secretary to help in his education, and his mother chose the texts to be read to him, opening her son's eyes, so to speak, to a world of enormous intellectual breadth, with the great works of Spanish literature at its centre. Rodrigo had his first music lessons – in sol-fa, piano and violin – at the age of 8 and enjoyed a rigorous training in Valencia in his teens. His first documented composition (a piano piece, now lost) dates from 1922 and, the year after, the floodgates seem to have opened, releasing a stream of music that flowed inexhaustibly for over 60 years.

Like many other Spanish composers in the first half of the 20th century, Rodrigo went north, to Paris, to complete his musical education and for five years studied with Paul Dukas. It was there, marooned for the duration of the Spanish Civil War, that he wrote the *Concierto de Aranjuez* before returning to Spain in 1939 after hostilities were over. *Aranjuez* was one of 14 concertante pieces that Rodrigo composed over the years, for a number of prominent soloists: the other piece in this year's Proms, the *Concierto pastoral*, was written to a commission from the flautist James Galway in 1977.

Rodrigo's energy made him an indispensable element in Spanish musical life: he was also an important critic and writer, and he held a startling number of administrative posts. Small wonder that his centenary is being fêted so widely at home and elsewhere – and, had he lived only two more years, he would have been here to enjoy the celebrations with us.

ABOVE
Joaquín Rodrigo, c1941

BELOW
Pete Postlethwaite as the leader of the fictional Grimley Colliery Band in Mark Herman's 1996 film *Brassed Off*, which featured a brass-band arrangement of the 'Orange Juice Concerto'

Rodrigo at the Proms

Prom 37 Concierto pastoral; Concierto de Aranjuez

ROYAL ACADEMY OF MUSIC

President: HRH The Duchess of Gloucester GCVO • Principal: Curtis Price

training versatile and resourceful professionals to the highest level

Britain's senior conservatoire, a full college of the University of London, enjoys a highly enviable location alongside Regent's Park. Our mission: **to prepare students for a successful career in music according to the evolving demands of the profession.**

- opening later this year, the York Gate Collections will for the first time provide public access to the Academy's superb collections of instruments, documents and artefacts

- significant additional facilities include a new 200-seat concert hall and top quality spaces for rehearsal and teaching

- a close-knit and truly international student community, with over 50 countries represented

  - guidance for students and recent graduates on how to get started in the profession

    - over 90% of recent Academy graduates have established their careers in music

      - an internationally renowned annual Composer Festival – in 2002 with György Kurtág, in collaboration with the South Bank Centre

      - Royal Academy Opera starts in 2001

      - a welcoming and dynamic working environment – why not drop in and have a look?

▸ **Marylebone Road, London NW1 5HT**
▸ **www.ram.ac.uk** ▸ **Tel. 020 7873 7373**

Michael Tilson Thomas
Conductor & Composer

Sibelius is the world's best-selling music notation software for Windows and Mac. It's easy to learn and fast to use, even if you're unfamiliar with computers. Sibelius notates, plays back and prints every type of music, from basic piano parts to complex orchestration. Used by top musicians and establishments such 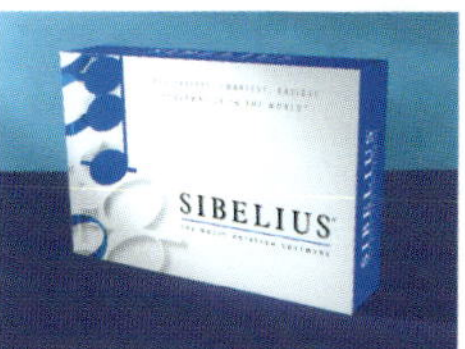 as Michael Tilson Thomas, the Royal Academy of Music and the BBC, it's ideal for composing, arranging, teaching and studying music. To find out just how quick and easy Sibelius is to use, call us on freephone **0800 458 3111** and ask for a free information pack and demo CD-ROM.

- Professional print quality.
- Fast and easy to learn.
- Write any kind of music.
- Instant layout: reformats a complete score in 1/10th of a second.
- Flexi-time™: intelligent real-time input.
- Scanning.
- Espressivo™: plays with realistic expression.
- Internet publishing.

SIBELIUS®

THE MUSIC NOTATION SOFTWARE

0800 458 3111
Fax: 01223 707101

www.sibelius.com
infoUK@sibelius.com

DECODERS WANTED.

As an RAF musician, your one advantage will be to decipher codes that even some of our top signal operators are baffled by. We are currently looking for single-reed woodwind instrumentalists, bassoonists and percussionists. So if you're aged between 17-29 and play the clarinet, bassoon or a percussion instrument to a professional standard and have always dreamt of playing for your country, just drop a note to: Squadron Leader Dave Compton ARCM (RAF), Director of Music (HQMS), RAF Uxbridge, Middlesex UB10 0RZ. Tel 01895 237144 ext. 6391. Or visit us at www.rafcareers.com or www.rafmusic.co.uk

BPG01

'There is nothing I long for more
intensely … than to be taken
for a better sort of Tchaikovsky –
for heaven's sake; a bit better,
but really that's all. Or if anything
more, then that people should know
my tunes and whistle them'
Schoenberg in a letter to Hans Rosbaud, 1947

Arnold Schoenberg (1874–1951)

Half a century after the Viennese composer's death, Ivan Hewett argues that there's more to the man and his music than his notorious 12-tone method

Some music may be born ahead of its time, but sooner or later the times catch up with it. The late quartets of Beethoven no longer scare us, Wagner's 'art-works of the future' sit comfortably in every opera house. But Arnold Schoenberg still awaits the era that will truly understand his music and take it to its heart. And perhaps he always will: his music will always be too modern for some and not modern enough for others.

Shortly after his death in 1951, Schoenberg was dismissed by the then 26-year-old Pierre Boulez as an irrelevance, a man who had glimpsed a brave new world but had lacked the courage to seize and colonise it. Fifty years later, his notorious 'serial' method is widely read and written about, routinely taught on music courses, but used by almost nobody. It's an ironic fate for the man who, in the mid-1920s, declared that his 12-tone system of composition 'would ensure the supremacy of German music for the next 100 years'.

Schoenberg needed the consoling prospect of long-term victory, as the present offered him nothing but defeat.

Even before the First World War, he was loathed as the perfect embodiment of the alienation and cacophony of modern music – despite the fact that, in his twenties, he had written works (such as the string sextet *Verklärte Nacht* or the choral epic *Gurrelieder*) that were the perfection of gorgeously ripe romanticism. Not only was Schoenberg always 'out of time', he was always 'out of place' – a Jew in Germany and Austria during the Nazi period; later, a German-speaking exile in California.

As if that weren't enough, a new problem arose in the 1920s when he started to compose with his '12-tone method'. The pieces he had written before – the so-called 'Expressionist' works like *Erwartung* and *Pierrot lunaire* – may have been full of frightening nightmare states expressed through dissonant shrieks, but at least the music was self-consistent. Whereas the new 'serial' music – in which every single note in a piece was determined by its place in an arbitrary sequence or 'series' of all 12 notes of the scale (rather than by the rules of conventional tonality) – seemed strangely divided against itself. The music surges with

expressive melody that often sounds like Brahms seen in a distorting mirror, yet the dissonant harmonies that accompany it equally often suggest the torments and anxieties of the era in which the music was written.

The '12-tone method' that Schoenberg invented to replace tonality may exact an iron control over every bar, yet the dense counterpoint, the ebb and flow of harmonic tension, and the procession of phrases and paragraphs all hark back to the great Austro-German tradition. This makes for a piquant mix of strict discipline and free fantasy, of heat and formality, that is the very essence of this music's fascination.

And yet, despite that, the image of Schoenberg as a cold systematiser of

51

music persists. Indeed, for some, Schoenberg's serial pieces can no longer be heard just as music, they're test-cases for the success or failure of his compositional system. It really is extraordinary how much energy Schoenberg's critics have devoted to trying to prove that we can't *hear* the series in his 'serial' music and that, even if we could, it still wouldn't make his music *sound* like music. But Schoenberg was well aware that the series by itself wouldn't make a piece comprehensible, and he took care to turn it into a proper theme à la Brahms (which is what irked Boulez, who thought this was back-sliding).

Yet all such attempts to show that Schoenberg 'got it wrong' surely miss the point. If he was simply a cold theoriser who came up with the wrong theory, people would turn from his music with a shrug of indifference. But they don't. If they can't love it, they rage against it – which shows that the real problem of Schoenberg's music isn't that it's cold but that it's far too hot.

There are other composers whose music has a similar fervid quality – above all, Tchaikovsky (with whom Schoenberg once wrote that he hoped to be compared). The difference is that, with Schoenberg, the emotional heat isn't expressed through yearning melodies and harmonies – or not just that. It's expressed through density and complexity of musical thought, just as it is in Bach or Beethoven or Brahms.

It was loyalty to the great tradition that led Schoenberg to invent his method in the first place. The binding force of tonality had loosened, and the strange new sounds unleashed in music – by many composers, but above all by him – were threatening to tear it apart. For Schoenberg, it was useless to deny this, and to try to recapture the past, as Stravinsky did. One had to face the inexorable demands of history, and invent a new system to replace the old.

Only that way could the tradition be renewed.

This is why Schoenberg insisted – though no-one believed him – that he was not a revolutionary. He was simply taking the inevitable next step, a step he took in the sure knowledge that it would earn him nothing but incomprehension and reproach. As he put it, 'Somebody had to be Schoenberg, and the lot fell to me.'

Schoenberg's real challenge to today's world is his refusal to compromise – and that is why we should love his music, and why his time is now. He expressed the agonising contradictions of his own age and his own character in music devoid of self-pity, but full of passionate intensity, rapt beauty, wit and, sometimes even, high good humour. It is music that offers a moral as well as a musical beacon.

Schoenberg at the Proms

Prom 17   Variations for
           Orchestra, Op. 31
Prom 38   De profundis;
           Friede auf Erden
Prom 40   Violin Concerto; Notturno
Prom 50   Pelleas and Melisande
Prom 51   Accompaniment to
           a Film Scene
Prom 59   Pierrot lunaire; Verklärte
           Nacht
Prom 67   A Survivor from Warsaw
PCM 4   Chamber Symphony No. 1
           (arr. Webern); arrangements
           of Busoni and J. Strauss II

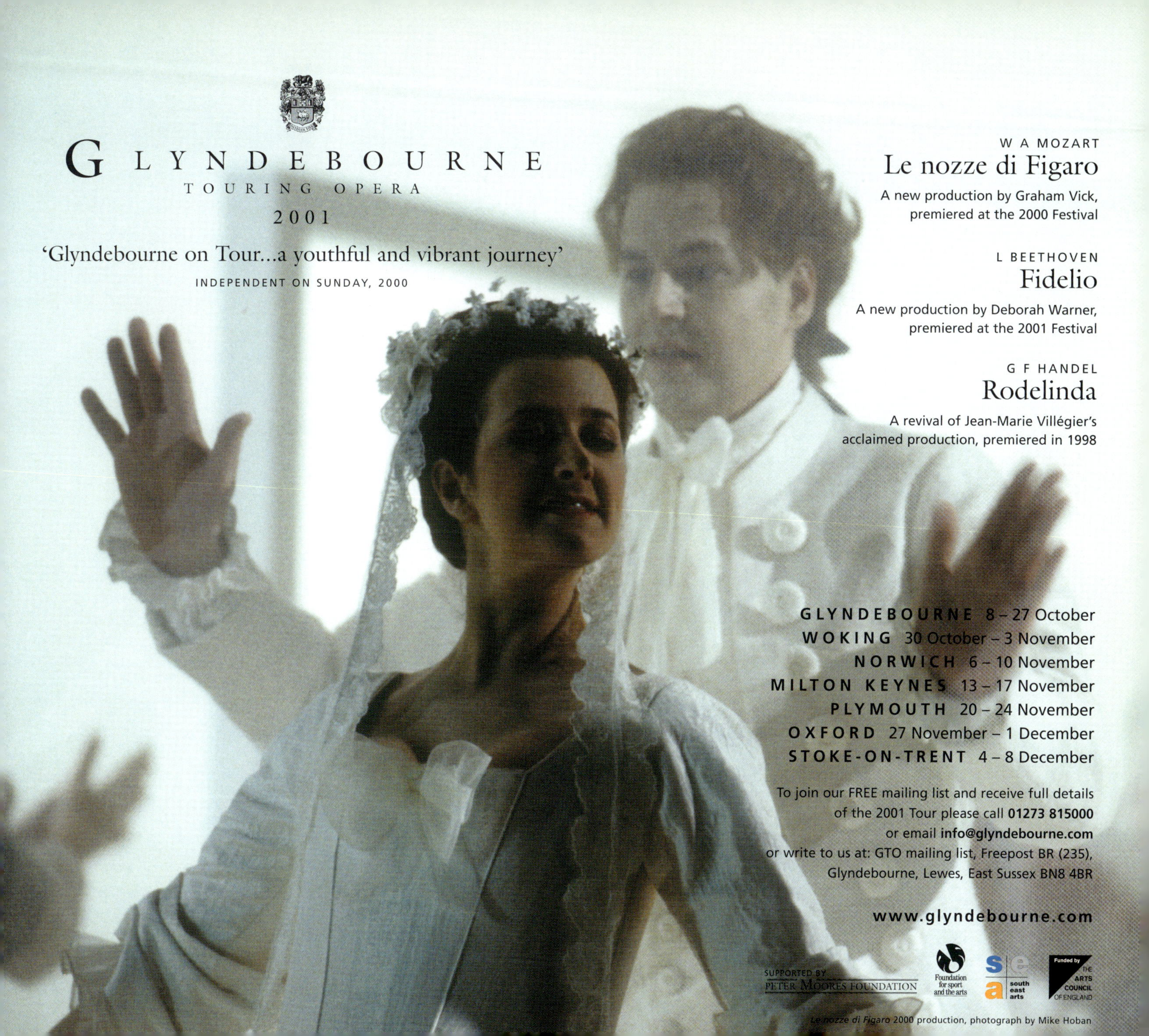

GLYNDEBOURNE
TOURING OPERA
2001

'Glyndebourne on Tour...a youthful and vibrant journey'

INDEPENDENT ON SUNDAY, 2000

W A MOZART
Le nozze di Figaro

A new production by Graham Vick,
premiered at the 2000 Festival

L BEETHOVEN
Fidelio

A new production by Deborah Warner,
premiered at the 2001 Festival

G F HANDEL
Rodelinda

A revival of Jean-Marie Villégier's
acclaimed production, premiered in 1998

GLYNDEBOURNE 8 – 27 October
WOKING 30 October – 3 November
NORWICH 6 – 10 November
MILTON KEYNES 13 – 17 November
PLYMOUTH 20 – 24 November
OXFORD 27 November – 1 December
STOKE-ON-TRENT 4 – 8 December

To join our FREE mailing list and receive full details
of the 2001 Tour please call **01273 815000**
or email **info@glyndebourne.com**
or write to us at: GTO mailing list, Freepost BR (235),
Glyndebourne, Lewes, East Sussex BN8 4BR

www.glyndebourne.com

SUPPORTED BY
PETER MOORES FOUNDATION

Le nozze di Figaro 2000 production, photograph by Mike Hoban

HISTORIC ROYAL PALACES

London's Historic Royal Palaces are considered by many to be the most beautifully preserved and fascinating buildings in Great Britain.

For hundreds of years the palaces of Kensington, Hampton Court, The Tower of London and The Banqueting House in Whitehall have provided a backdrop for the drama and pageantry of the British Monarchy.

As befitting their great entertainment traditions of the past, The Historic Royal Palaces are available for corporate and charitable functions. Each of these unique palaces is able to provide a setting for a wide range of formal events, whether a lavish banquet or an intimate dinner for a select few.

Whether you choose to enjoy a reception in the famous Hall of Monarchs before a private view of the breathtaking crown jewels at The Tower of London; to dine in the splendour of Henry VIII's Great Hall at Hampton Court Palace; to hold a reception under the splendid Rubens ceiling at the Banqueting House Whitehall Palace or to dine in the serene and elegant Orangery at Kensington Palace, you will appreciate that few venues can match the grandeur, style and sheer diversity of The Historic Royal Palaces.

For more information about the use of these palaces, please contact the functions departments at the relevant palace.

HM Tower of London 020 7488 5762

Hampton Court Palace 020 8781 9508

Kensington Palace 020 7376 2452

The Banqueting House Whitehall Palace 020 7839 8919

Historic Royal Palaces Enterprises Ltd
www.hrp.org.uk

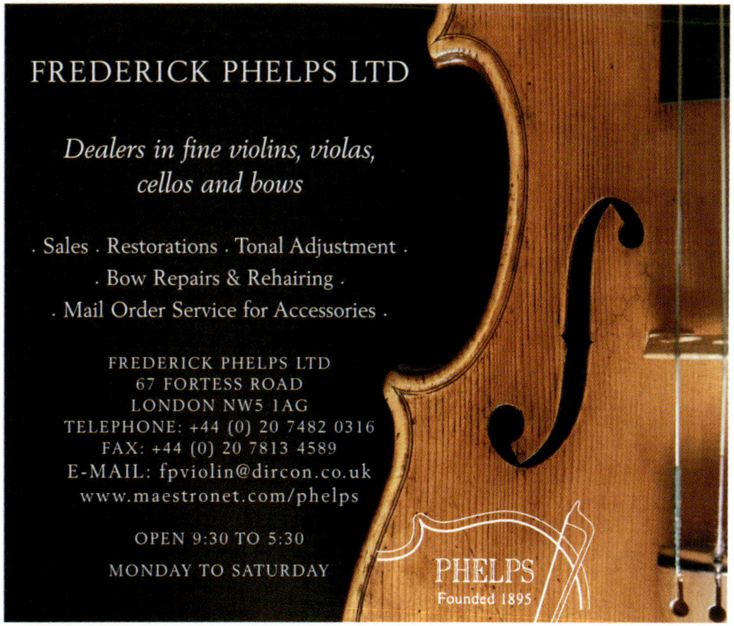
FREDERICK PHELPS LTD
Dealers in fine violins, violas, cellos and bows
. Sales . Restorations . Tonal Adjustment .
. Bow Repairs & Rehairing .
. Mail Order Service for Accessories .
FREDERICK PHELPS LTD
67 FORTESS ROAD
LONDON NW5 1AG
TELEPHONE: +44 (0) 20 7482 0316
FAX: +44 (0) 20 7813 4589
E-MAIL: fpviolin@dircon.co.uk
www.maestronet.com/phelps
OPEN 9:30 TO 5:30
MONDAY TO SATURDAY
PHELPS
Founded 1895

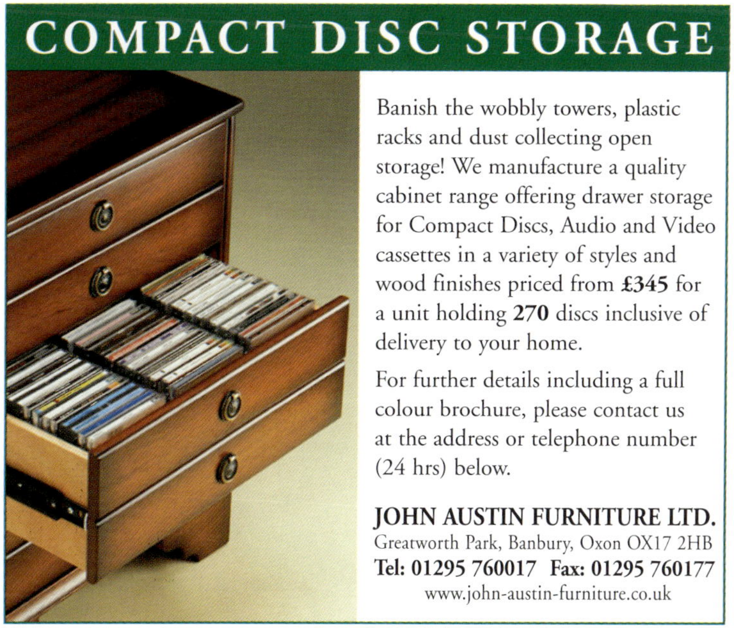
COMPACT DISC STORAGE
Banish the wobbly towers, plastic racks and dust collecting open storage! We manufacture a quality cabinet range offering drawer storage for Compact Discs, Audio and Video cassettes in a variety of styles and wood finishes priced from £345 for a unit holding 270 discs inclusive of delivery to your home.
For further details including a full colour brochure, please contact us at the address or telephone number (24 hrs) below.
JOHN AUSTIN FURNITURE LTD.
Greatworth Park, Banbury, Oxon OX17 2HB
Tel: 01295 760017 Fax: 01295 760177
www.john-austin-furniture.co.uk

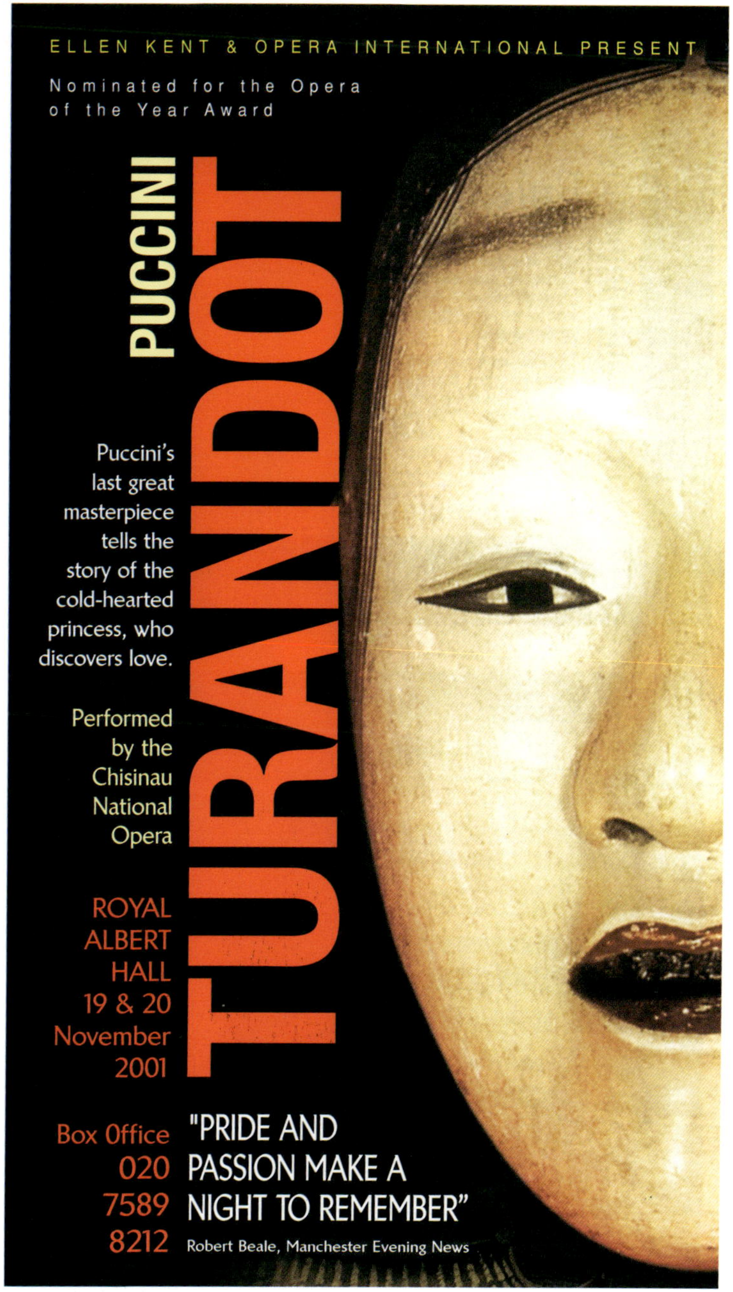
ELLEN KENT & OPERA INTERNATIONAL PRESENT
Nominated for the Opera of the Year Award
PUCCINI
TURANDOT
Puccini's last great masterpiece tells the story of the cold-hearted princess, who discovers love.
Performed by the Chisinau National Opera
ROYAL ALBERT HALL
19 & 20 November 2001
Box Office 020 7589 8212
"PRIDE AND PASSION MAKE A NIGHT TO REMEMBER"
Robert Beale, Manchester Evening News

Erard, Paris, 1914

PERIOD PIANO COMPANY
Unique Instruments

Park Farm Oast, Hareplain Rd. Biddenden, KENT TN27 8LJ
tel/FAX (01580) 291393 email: periodpiano@talk21.com
www.periodpiano.com

John Myatt Woodwind & Brass

The UK's premier wind instrument specialist

FREE
56 page catalogue, regularly updated special offer and secondhand lists or visit our web site

ALL REEDS SENT FIRST CLASS POST FREE!!!
10% DISCOUNT FOR ORDERS of 5 BOXES (any combination) or 5 BASSOON OR OBOE REEDS!!!

Extensive stocks of new & secondhand instruments and accessories

Competitive prices

Specialist knowledge

Friendly, efficient service

Professional set up on ALL instruments - Comprehensive guarantee

Rental scheme - Specialist educational supplier

John Myatt Woodwind & Brass
57 Nightingale Road, Hitchin, Herts SG5 1RQ
Tel: +44 (0)1462 420057
Fax: +44 (0)1462 435464
shop@myatt.co.uk • www.myatt.co.uk

JOHN MYATT
WOODWIND & BRASS SPECIALISTS

BRITISH RESERVE
Insurance

SPECIALIST INSURER
OF MUSICAL INSTRUMENTS

Competitive premiums
to suit all music-makers:

• Amateurs and professionals
• World renowned virtuosi
• Orchestras
• Young musicians

Quotes - direct from us on
0870 2400 303 (stating Ref.BBC)
... or from your usual dealer

British Reserve Insurance is part
of the Cornhill group
Sponsor of the Classic FM Music
Teacher of the Year Award

British Reserve Insurance Co. Ltd.
Musical Instruments Department
Cornhill House, 6 Vale Avenue
Tunbridge Wells
Kent TN1 1EH

Fax: 0870 1600 304
E-mail: BRIC@cornhill.co.uk
Website:www.britishreserve.co.uk

SC1716/2

Weill • Royal Palace

Erik Levi introduces a 'lost' Weimar opera by Kurt Weill, written in the years before he met Bertolt Brecht

Although the BBC Symphony Orchestra's highly acclaimed *Berlin to Broadway* festival at the Barbican in January 2000 introduced British audiences to a number of Kurt Weill's previously unknown works, none was more intriguing than the one-act opera *Royal Palace*. Composed in 1927, just after Weill had established a burgeoning reputation as a theatre composer with *Der Protagonist*, *Royal Palace* marks a significant departure from his earlier expressionist style. Following the fashion for topicality then current in Weimar theatre, it is a fully-fledged *Zeitoper* ('Opera of its time') with spectacular musical and scenic effects, including a film sequence – the first use of such technology on the operatic stage.

The libretto, by the surrealist poet Iwan Goll, is no less remarkable than the music. Drawing its inspiration from Greek mythology, it transports the characters of Orpheus and Dejanira, the estranged wife of Heracles, into the modern world, but with consequences that often descend into parody. The setting is a luxurious hotel on the edge of an Italian lake where three men, the Husband, Yesterday's Lover and Tomorrow's Admirer, compete desperately with each other to try and secure Dejanira's love. The Husband showers her with material possessions, arranging an exotic dinner and presenting a film that illustrates his wife's jet-setting lifestyle – holidaying in Nice, travelling on the Orient Express, flying to the North Pole in an aircraft. Yesterday's Lover counters this with a nocturnal, erotic fantasy and a ballet of the constellations, while Tomorrow's Admirer conjures up a timeless vision of the future in which Orpheus leads a group of animals into the distance. Dejanira, however, rejects each suitor on the grounds of their selfishness, before renouncing the world and throwing herself into the lake. In the opera's extended tango-finale, Dejanira is transformed into a mermaid, while her Husband cries out in disbelief at the events that have just taken place.

First staged at the Berlin State Opera under Erich Kleiber, *Royal Palace* was withdrawn after only seven performances. Tragically, the full score and all the performance materials disappeared after 1929, and the opera had to be reconstructed through orchestration of the published vocal score, a task undertaken by the American composer Gunther Schuller in 1971. Yet last year's British premiere of the work by the BBC proved to be a revelation, showing on the one hand an unexpected predilection for late-Romantic opulence in the manner of Franz Schreker and, on the other, a striking incorporation of 1920s popular dance rhythms into the musical fabric – an ingredient that was to become even more crucial in Weill's subsequent and better-known collaborations with Bertolt Brecht.

Weill • Royal Palace
Prom 17 Thursday 2 August, 7.30pm

ABOVE
Kurt Weill in 1936

RIGHT
Royal Palace: scene from the premiere production at the Berlin State Opera in 1927

BELOW
Royal Palace: poster for the 1927 premiere

Grieg • Music for 'Peer Gynt'

Irving Wardle explains that Grieg's music is more than merely incidental to the dramatic success of Ibsen's great play

Well before Ibsen's *Peer Gynt* arrived on the international stage Grieg's *Peer Gynt* Suites were old favourites on the European concert platform: a fact not always relished by the Ibsen lobby. 'Few musical scores,' writes his biographer Michael Meyer, 'can have so softened an author's intentions as Grieg's … which turns the play into a jolly Hans Andersen fairy tale.' Bernard Shaw, too, began by patronising Grieg's 'trivial' additions to his hero's masterpiece, but then had to acknowledge that at least they developed 'according to the logic' of Ibsen's scenes.

That is the crucial point: what Grieg produced was true theatre music. This is not evident from the familiar Suites, which consist of self-sufficient numbers presented out of dramatic sequence, but becomes apparent in complete performances of Ibsen's play, like Tyrone Guthrie's legendary 1944 production starring Ralph Richardson, or in presentations, like that at this year's Proms, where you can encounter Grieg and Ibsen on more equal terms.

Ibsen himself had proposed splitting the profits 50/50 when he first invited Grieg to compose the incidental music for his play's premiere. For the allegedly unmusical author, such a commission was a necessary move in adapting his vast dramatic poem for a public not yet accustomed to continuous spoken drama.

In the event, the 1876 premiere in Christiania (now Oslo) was a success. Before the event, however, the signs were ominous. Grieg took small pleasure in the work; finding the subject 'unmanageable' and 'unmusical', and declaring his own Troll music (known in the Suites as 'In the Hall of the Mountain King') to be so 'full of cow-turds' that he couldn't bear to listen to it. How, in any case, could one expect a successful partnership between a Romantic nationalist like Grieg and the émigré Ibsen, who thought the best thing for his homeland would be for it to sink into the sea?

The answer lies in the two men's shared absorption in Norwegian folk legend and folk song, with both text and music tapping into sources beyond self-expression so that they inhabit the same world without duplicating one another's effects. Shaw thought Grieg missed the point by failing to reinforce Peer's farewell speech to his dying mother, Åse, with an orchestral sleigh-ride. That

Edvard Grieg: statue at Troldhaugen, Norway

would have been no more than a redundant caption. What we get instead – a spoken childhood fantasy plus a three-note elegy – is the combination that grips the mind and heart. Context is all. Solveig's Song transcends lyricism by appearing immediately after Peer's betrayal of Anitra, the Moorish enchantress; the Night Music becomes a secular *Dies irae* for the aged Peer; and at his meeting with the Boyg, the voice of Peer's fate, a single prolonged note stretches out towards the frozen landscapes of Sibelius and Musorgsky's bare mountain. This is the work of two great dramatists.

Grieg • Music for 'Peer Gynt'
Prom 27 Thursday 9 August, 7.30pm

BELOW

Solveig and Åse await Peer's return: detail from Edvard Munch's poster for a Paris performance of *Peer Gynt* in 1896

Messiaen • Turangalîla Symphony

Julian Anderson outlines the intimate origins of the French composer's massive 10-movement 'song of love and hymn of joy'

Messiaen was never a composer to do things by half. Asked by Koussevitzky to write a work for the Boston Symphony Orchestra 'of any size and length you wish', he came up with a piece in 10 movements, lasting 75 minutes, scored for a huge orchestra with both solo piano and solo ondes martenot (that strangely wailing French electronic instrument invented between the wars).

The subject-matter turned out to be equally extravagant. According to Messiaen, the Sanskrit *turangalîla* is composed of two words: *turanga*, meaning the passing or flow of time, and *lîla*, meaning the play of life, love and death. The combination of these two words results in 'a song of love and a hymn of joy'. The *Turangalîla-symphonie* was the second work in Messiaen's so-called 'Tristan trilogy', a group of three pieces from the 1940s dealing with the idea of 'an irresistible, fatal love, a love which inevitably leads directly to death'.

This was perhaps a surprising subject for a composer closely associated with the Catholic Church. A clue to its origins was given later by Messiaen himself. He recalled the 1940s as 'the period in which I had most inspiration', a fact he explained in poetic but unusually personal terms: 'Birds sing at many times of the year, but they sing best in spring, the season of love … Perhaps this is the explanation, because this was the period when Yvonne Loriod came into my life.'

Since 1943 Messiaen had already produced over four hours of music featuring Loriod's brilliant pianistic talents. But in *Turangalîla* he wrote for

her not only his most virtuosic piano part to date, but also a work of extraordinary colour, tenderness and joy, containing the most overt love music he ever penned. (Messiaen graphically named the work's two main themes 'the statue' and 'the flower'.) Messiaen and Loriod eventually married, and most of his later major works continued to feature her as soloist.

The Boston Symphony gave the work's first performance in 1949, not under Koussevitzky, who was ill, but under the young Leonard Bernstein. Whatever his opinion of *Turangalîla*, Bernstein never conducted it again. Indeed, it is a curious fact that, despite its quick success with audiences, Messiaen's symphony went down less well with the musical fraternity. One major composer simply dismissed it as 'trash', while Pierre Boulez, Messiaen's own star pupil, famously labelled it 'bordello music'.

The affection in which *Turangalîla* is held by audiences has never dimmed, however. Admittedly, its blatantly tonal explosions of love music sit oddly next to the complex, mathematically inspired polyrhythms, the shrill haze of cluster harmonies, the clicking and crashing of the percussion. But today, when there is more talk of musical pluralism and cross-cultural fertilisation, *Turangalîla* can be seen as an astonishingly prophetic work, perhaps more thoroughly daring in its attempt at fusing cultures and musics than anything attempted since.

Messiaen • Turangalîla Symphony
Prom 29 Saturday 11 August, 7.00pm

Beethoven • Fidelio

David Cairns trumpets the universal truths of Beethoven's only opera, brought to this year's Proms by Glyndebourne Festival

The 19th-century novelist Thomas Love Peacock, reviewing the opera's first London performance, summed up the qualities that make Beethoven's *Fidelio* unique. In it, he said, the expression of emotion is carried 'to a pitch scarcely conceivable'. 'The playfulness of youthful hope, the heroism of devoted love, the rage of the tyrant, the despair of the captive, the bursting of the sunshine of liberty upon the gloom of the dungeon … are portrayed in music not merely with truth of expression as that term might be applied to other works, but with a force and reality that makes music an intelligible language' – a language which, Peacock added, 'speaks to the soul'.

These qualities are enhanced by a good staging: well directed and well acted, the moment in the dungeon scene when Leonore (disguised as the youth Fidelio) points her pistol at Pizarro, the corrupt prison governor, and seems actually to produce the trumpet call which rings out faint but clear from high above, signalling her husband's impending liberation, remains one of the most thrilling in all opera. But the work can exert the same spell away from the theatre, whether in the concert hall or in the kind of semi-staging that Glyndebourne traditionally brings to the Proms. *Fidelio* needs elaborate production less than almost any other music-drama. Its 'force and reality' impose their own laws, their own world, and take possession of performers and audience alike.

Beethoven's only opera has not invariably enjoyed critical approval. The years of labour it cost him, and the unorthodox form of the work, have been used to prove that the supreme symphonic composer was unsuited to the

theatre. Certainly, he goes his own way, with the same disregard of categories and convention as in his symphonies. The opera begins as domestic comedy, graduates to heroic melodrama, and culminates as a kind of cantata.

It has the best possible reasons for doing so. *Fidelio* celebrates not only one particular woman's fearless love but the universal human virtues of courage, devotion, faith, hatred of injustice – qualities which may spring up anywhere, in the most apparently hopeless surroundings, or in the most humdrum and banal. Hence both the all-consuming blaze of sound which ends the work and the homely tone of the opening scenes. The power and psychological truthfulness of the dungeon scene have never been denied; but equally masterly is the pacing of the first act, the way the musical language gradually deepens and intensifies as the drama nears its goal.

By the end of all his revisions and simplifyings (the opera went through three distinct versions between 1805 and 1814), Beethoven had achieved an orchestral sonority, harsh but glowing, which exactly embodied the work's message of suffering transcended by love – a sonority that will surely be all the more striking when rendered, as at Glyndebourne's Proms performance, on the period instruments of the Orchestra of the Age of Enlightenment.

Beethoven · Fidelio
Prom 35 Thursday 16 August, 7.30pm

ABOVE
The statue of Beethoven in Münsterplatz, Bonn (the composer's birthplace)

LEFT
Wilhelmine Schröder-Devrient as Leonore (lithograph by W. Santer): the most famous Fidelio of the 19th century, she had studied the role with Beethoven himself. Wagner, who saw her perform it when he was 16, later praised her for singing 'more with the soul than with the voice'

Bartók • Duke Bluebeard's Castle

Paul Griffiths looks to Bartók (and Boulez)
for some musical marriage guidance

Bartók wrote his one-act opera *Duke Bluebeard's Castle* in 1911 (the year of his 30th birthday) and gave it as a wedding-present to his first wife. She might well have been unsettled by the gift, for in the opera Judith arrives with her new husband Bluebeard at his dank, dark and gloomy castle, only to find it full of doors which he seems reluctant to open. As she gradually succeeds in prising the keys from him and unlocking the doors, she discovers that Bluebeard's silence hid more than she was prepared for …

She discovers his treasure, his weaponry, his vast domains, but on everything she sees bloodstains, the pain and suffering he has created in his own life and that of others. Behind the sixth door is a lake of tears, a vision of the man's interior landscape. After that, all possibility of a relationship between them is over. The seventh door opens to reveal all Bluebeard's former wives, whom Judith joins, the latest shadow in his past.

At this relatively early point in his career, Bartók was still indebted to his elder contemporaries, especially Richard Strauss and Debussy, and his orchestral score for *Duke Bluebeard's Castle* is full of colour and character, of grand sweeps and intense points of detail, while the two characters sing out their story in a manner that is all the more poignant for its understatement. Since there is little action beyond the opening of the seven doors, this is an opera that works very well as theatre for the mind's eye – as Pierre Boulez and the BBC Symphony Orchestra, who present the work at this year's Proms, have regularly shown in concert performances together since the early Seventies.

Boulez's own *Le visage nuptial* ('The Wedded Face'), which he conducts in the concert's first half, is an even more youthful piece than Bartók's opera: he wrote it when he was just 21, setting dense and passionate poetry by René Char. Both works describe impossible marriages. Whereas Bartók's characters are newly-weds, immediately flung apart because she needs to go beyond the limits of what he will let her know, in Boulez's cantata the immoderate force is love itself – love that grabs people in its hand and crushes them. The voices in Bartók's opera are those of people in an allegorical but still concrete situation. Boulez's voices are those of souls on fire.

ABOVE
Pierre Boulez

LEFT
Portrait of Duke Bluebeard by János Kass (born 1927): one of a series of 10 pictures (dated 1960–90) inspired by Bartók's opera

Bartók • Duke Bluebeard's Castle
Boulez • Le visage nuptial
Prom 51 Wednesday 29 August, 7.00pm

Music AT CHRIST'S HOSPITAL

HMC Co-educational Boarding School 11 - 18
Horsham West Sussex RH13 7YP

"Outstanding. First rate music" Daily Telegraph Good Schools Guide
"One of the top two co-educational schools for music in the country"
Classic FM Magazine

Christ's Hospital has one of the largest music departments in the country, offering exceptional tuition and magnificent facilities within the framework of an excellent and broad education.

- **Music Awards available at age 11, 13 (for choristers), 16.**
- **Currently, 38% of pupils receive free education, according to parental income.**
- **Open Afternoon: Saturday 6 October 2001.**

For a Prospectus call

01403 211293

www.christs-hospital.org.uk

Reg. Charity No. 306975

> Make Music Your Future

In Summer 2001, Trinity College of Music re-locates to the Old Royal Naval College in Greenwich to continue its excellence in provision of performance and pedagogy training.

To request a prospectus of undergraduate, postgraduate, foundation studies contact:

Trinity College of Music
11–13 Mandeville Place
London W1M 6AQ
Tel +44 (0)20 7935 5773 Fax +44 (0)20 7224 6278
E-mail info@tcm.ac.uk or visit the Website http://www.tcm.ac.uk

registered charity no.309998

TRINITY
college of music

National Children's Orchestra

established 1978

for talented children aged between 7 & 13

. . . the standard they achieved was astonishing, to say the least.
Press comment

- Five age-banded orchestras •
- Three regional orchestras for members •
- Easter and summer holiday courses • Autumn auditions •
- Members come from all parts of the British Isles •
- Coaching by leading musicians •

Details from: Roger Clarkson, Director of Music
84a Elm Tree Road, Locking, Weston-super-Mare, North Somerset BS24 8EH
Tel: 01934 820254   Fax: 01934 820257
E-mail: mail@nco.org.uk   Website: www.nco.org.uk

ELY FUND MANAGERS LIMITED

Specialists in the management of bespoke
investment portfolios for private clients.
We also look after family trusts,
charities and pensions.

For more information, contact Rollo Duckworth

AUDREY HOUSE • ELY PLACE • LONDON EC1N 6SN

Tel: 020 7404 5333

www.ely.uk.com

Regulated by IMRO

symphony hall
birmingham

2001
ten years of making great music

10

'Symphony Hall never fails to surprise the ears and delight the spirits'
The Times, February 2001

'an inspiration to the orchestra...an inspiration also to its audiences'
The Times

'The best concert hall in the country'
Daily Telegraph

box office 0121 780 3333
www.symphonyhall.co.uk/symphony admin tel: +44 (0)121 200 2000
fax: +44 (0)121 212 1982 email: symphonyhall@necgroup.co.uk

INVESCO

11th Century
12th Century
13th Century
14th Century
16th Century
17th Century
18th Century
19th Century
20th Century

Hitting the right notes for the 21st Century investor

Music has provided pleasure for generation after generation.
Take a look back 1,000 years. Take the leap forward to the 21st Century, with INVESCO.

INVESCO

At the dawn of the new millennium, let INVESCO be your guide to the world of investment for the 21st Century.

From Unit Trusts and ISAs to Investment Trusts and Portfolio Management – INVESCO – choosing the right note for all your investment needs.

www.invesco.co.uk

Call us on free on 0800 028 4050

Please quote reference: 123911

INVESCO Fund Managers Limited. 11 Devonshire Square, London EC2M 4YR. E-mail: client.services@invesco.co.uk Client Services: 0800 028 4050 Unit Trust Dealing: 0800 028 5522
Regulated by IMRO and the Personal Investment Authority and is a member of AUTIF. ISAs and Investment Trusts are provided by INVESCO Asset Management Limited, regulated by IMRO. Members of the AMVESCAP Group.

PP07.01

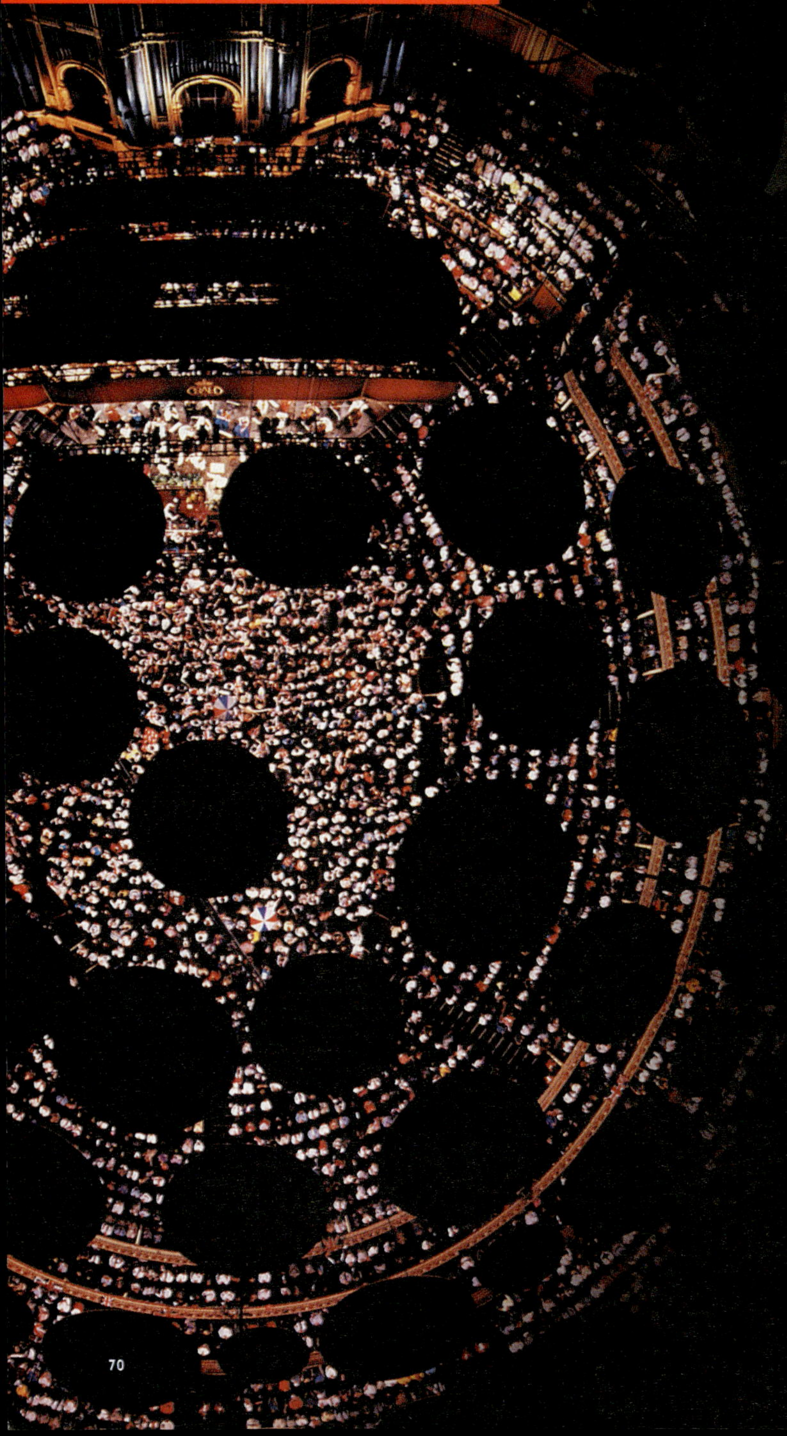

Proms Commissions and Premieres

For more than a century, the Proms have led the way in presenting new music. In his 50 years as the concerts' conductor, Henry Wood (*below*) personally premiered over 700 new works by more than 350 composers, while many now-popular pieces by Tchaikovsky, Mahler, Stravinsky, Elgar and others were first introduced to the British public at the Proms. The tradition continues this year with a tally of 10 BBC commissions and another 11 world, UK and London premieres – all explored here by David Threasher

BBC COMMISSION

Sally Beamish (b. 1956)

Knotgrass Elegy

World premiere • Prom 12

Sally Beamish's largest work to date is an oratorio bringing together elements as diverse as a jazz saxophone and a children's chorus to the usual cast of soloists, chorus and orchestra. Inspired by Graham Harvey's book *The Killing of the Countryside* and set in a latter-day Garden of Eden, the work describes the ravaging of our planet by pesticides and herbicides, with a particular focus on the fate of the humble knotgrass weed. The villain of the piece, of course, is the 'tempter', who deals out alluring agri-chemical cocktails, and the work describes a catalogue of destruction that results in the demise of both the knotgrass beetle and the partridge.

BBC COMMISSION

Sir Harrison Birtwistle (b. 1934)

New work

World premiere • Prom 64

Once an *enfant terrible* of the Sixties avant-garde, Harrison Birtwistle, now knighted and part of the establishment, continues to prove he can still shock, with works such as *Panic*, which memorably caused consternation at its premiere at the 1995 Last Night. The continuing success of his opera *The Last Supper* and February's 'composer portrait' concert presented by the BBC Symphony Orchestra are testimony to the power and range of his music; this Late Night Prom presents two sides of his recent work, with the Three Latin Motets from his millennial opera juxtaposed against his fanfare *Sonance*, and this brand new work for brass ensemble.

BBC COMMISSION

John Casken (b. 1949)

To the Lovers' Well

World premiere • PCM 7

A frequent visitor to the Proms, John Casken's first Proms performance was in 1986, with the 'Northumbrian Elegy' *To fields we do not know*. Over the intervening decade-and-a-half his music has returned every three years – and three years ago the Albert Hall saw the London premiere of his *Maharal Dreaming*, composed as a spin-off from his opera *Golem*. His commission for this year's Proms sets texts by Geoffrey Hill. 'The sequence of poems brings together themes of regeneration, death, birth, pain, healing and the wounded heart,' relates Casken, 'all within the symbolic setting of a landscape both green and rocky, where thorn and fruit, pain and desire are found side by side.'

BBC COMMISSION

Alexander Goehr (b. 1932)

… second musical offering (GFH 2001)

World premiere • Prom 67

Following on from his *… a musical offering (JSB 1985)*, composed for the Bach tercentenary, Alexander Goehr presents a second musical gift to Bach's exact contemporary, Handel. Goehr's preoccupation with the fusion of modernism and Baroque forms and practices – plus his continuing interest in Bachian numerology and even his own take on figured bass technique – is reflected in a long line of works, reaching through his operas *Behold the Sun* and *Arianna* to the present. This two-movement *hommage* – an 'Overture with Handelian Air' and a 'Concerto and Double' – casts contemporary glances at Handel's music. Goehr says, 'I believe that a close relationship to particular works of a now distant past can contribute to the forming of new rhetoric and new expressions in our own time.'

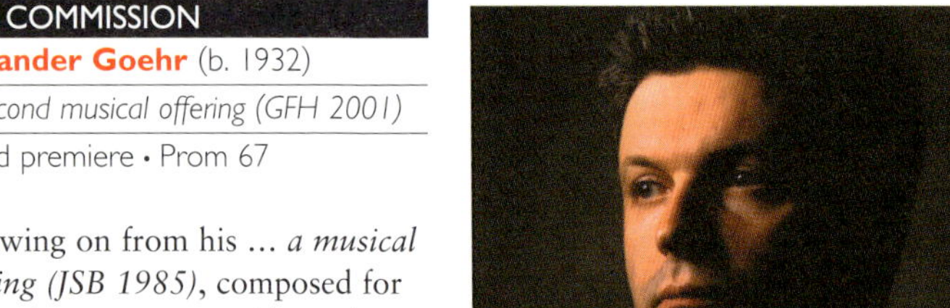

BBC COMMISSION

James MacMillan (b. 1959)

Birds of Rhiannon

World premiere • Prom 8

James MacMillan began his appointment as Composer/Conductor to the BBC Philharmonic last September to stunning reviews. His latest work for the orchestra is *Birds of Rhiannon* – 'mystical, angelic presences,' MacMillan explains, 'which appear and sing on the death of Bran – a Fisher King-type figure who sacrifices his life for the sake of peace between two warring peoples'. He describes the work as 'a dramatic concerto for orchestra with a mystical coda for choir' – supplied for this premiere by the voices of The Sixteen. MacMillan takes as his text a poem by Michael Symmons Roberts based on a story from the *Mabinogion*, the medieval collection of Welsh mythology.

BBC COMMISSION

Colin Matthews (b. 1946)

Fanfare

World premiere • Prom 1

Last year Colin Matthews gave us a tantalising glimpse of Pluto, in his 'completion' of Holst's ever-popular suite *The Planets*. This year we hear his orchestration of the overture which Benjamin Britten sketched out for his American operetta *Paul Bunyan* but cut before the work's 1941 premiere. As a curtain-raiser to this – and indeed to the whole of Proms 2001 – Matthews, once memorably described as the 'Isambard Kingdom Brunel of music', has applied his industry and craftsmanship to the miniature form of the fanfare in order to inaugurate Leonard Slatkin's first Prom as Chief Conductor of the BBC SO.

BBC COMMISSION

Julian Philips (b. 1969)

Out of Light

World premiere • Prom 57

Following on from his first orchestral work, *Strange Seas*, commissioned by the Britten Sinfonia and subsequently taken up by the BBC National Orchestra of Wales, Julian Philips describes his new work, *Out of Light*, as a symphonic journey 'out of light into darkness', with two waves of musical energy – one bright and diatonic, the other dark and unstable. 'For me,' explains Welsh-born Philips, 'its composition drew inspiration from the process of maturation that occurs in the transition from youth into adulthood. But my intention is that listeners should find their own private resonance and meaning in the purely musical events that unfold in the piece.'

BBC COMMISSION

Tobias Picker (b. 1954)

Cello Concerto

World premiere • Prom 30

When New Yorker Tobias Picker was asked to compose his Cello Concerto, he was already hard at work on another piece for the same instrument – a Suite for cello and piano, written especially for Lynn Harrell. The Concerto has been composed for Paul Watkins, who was Principal Cellist of the BBC SO for seven years from the age of 20. Picker's angular counterpoint drifts in and out of tonality, and with the immediacy of his musical language he has managed to marry something of the rigorous romanticism of Brahms with the detached, visceral rhythms of Stravinsky. Following the success of his first two operas, *Emmeline* and *Fantastic Mr. Fox*, Picker is now under commission to both Dallas Opera and the New York Metropolitan to write two new operas based respectively on Zola's *Thérèse Raquin* and Dreiser's *An American Tragedy*.

BBC/DANISH NATIONAL RADIO SO COMMISSION

Poul Ruders (b. 1949)

Studium (Double Percussion Concerto)

UK premiere • Prom 28

The Safri Duo have recently been reaching a wider audience, appearing on the BBC's *Top of the Pops* with their dance hit *Played A Live (The Bongo Song)*. Currently working on a dance album, they bring their 1.6 tons of percussion instruments to the Proms for Poul Ruders's concerto for double percussion, *Studium*. Ruders, currently basking in the recent success of his opera *The Handmaid's Tale*, describes *Studium* as an étude based on tight and sparse material, in which a huge structure is meticulously and patiently built. The virtuosity of the percussion increases, while the orchestra maintains its tightly-composed 'surround sound'. What happens then, says the composer, must remain a surprise!

BBC COMMISSION
Ian Wilson (b. 1964)

Man-o'-War

World premiere • Prom 23

'I wanted it to be energetic, and to explore deeper timbres and registers, and I was looking at all sorts of things like Robert Motherwell paintings, for instance, to try and find a context for my embryonic ideas,' says Belfast-born Ian Wilson of his Proms debut work. 'Anyway, the word "man-o'-war" leapt out at me one day, with its different connotations – an old word for a warship, also a very poisonous sea creature, and even a village not far from Dublin. So I'm attempting to combine these various elements – something martial, something to be taken seriously, something dangerous as well as an overall defining sense of character, like a defining sense of place.'

John Adams (b. 1947)

Naive and Sentimental Music

UK premiere • Prom 62

'Naive' and 'Sentimental' – words which may now bear connotations different from Schiller's when he first used them in the title to a now-forgotten essay over 200 years ago. Adams typically plays on their polarity, pitting naive music – instinctive music, music from within – against sentimental music – subjective music, dependent on outside influence. The work is dedicated to Esa-Pekka Salonen, who, as conductor and composer, is an embodiment of the dichotomy: composer – introvert, 'naive'; conductor – extrovert, 'sentimental'. Adams himself acknowledges that the 'naive' can only exist, like the fox's grapes, as an unreachable ideal, with too much 'sentimental' historical debris through which to wade.

Leonard Bernstein (1918–90)

West Side Story – Suite, orch. Brohn

UK premiere • Prom 18

West Side Story a premiere? It's over 40 years old, has had a recent West End run and is a mainstay of the amateur dramatic repertoire! But Bernstein's estate has sanctioned this arrangement of songs from the musical for orchestra and the violin of Joshua Bell, and it makes an admirable concert partner for the same composer's *Serenade*, also for violin and orchestra. Bell's Bernstein foray follows hard on the heels of his *Gershwin Fantasy* – and, as well as *West Side Story*, he has also tackled William David Brohn's arrangements from *On the Town*, and a version of 'Make Our Garden Grow' from *Candide*, specially prepared for him by John Corigliano.

Pierre Boulez (b. 1925)

Notations VII

UK premiere • Prom 30

Boulez is the past master of the 'work-in-progress' – and the latest in his projected series of orchestral *Notations* (of which the first four were heard at the Proms in 1999) is one of the most recent of his reworkings. Boulez's original *Notations* were composed for piano in 1945, during his student days with Messiaen, and are a set of 12 works, each 12 bars long – 12 being the *numéro-du-jour* in modernist times past. The orchestrations build on the piano pieces – a 12-bar orchestral work would clearly be perverse – expanding, amplifying and revisiting the work's ideas, so that the original single-page, one-minute miniature blossoms into a work eight times as long, for a massive orchestra. In Boulez's words: 'The seeds were there, far away, and then I began to conceive these as seeds for new thinking; for new development. And so it began.'

Michel Camilo (b. 1954)

Piano Concerto

UK premiere • Prom 45

Born in the Dominican Republic, Michel Camilo is best known to jazz-lovers the world over for his brilliant and original synthesis of jazz and effervescent Caribbean rhythms, propelled by an infectious, contemporary sense of swing. Among his influences he lists musicians ranging from Art Tatum and Oscar Peterson to Keith Jarrett and Erroll Garner – as well as Beethoven, Chopin and Debussy. His Piano Concerto has been taken up and championed by the BBC Symphony Orchestra's new Chief Conductor, Leonard Slatkin, who has already directed it in Cleveland with the composer at the keyboard, and here brings it to London for the first time.

Henryk Górecki (b. 1933)

Salve, sidus polonorum

UK premiere • Prom 38

Fame and fortune visited Henryk Górecki late in life – 'accidentally and bemusingly', according to the new *New Grove* – when his *Symphony of Sorrowful Songs* captured the ears of the music-loving world. Since then his reputation has rested primarily on his choral music, with such perfectly-wrought miniatures as the meditative *Totus tuus*. His new three-movement cantata *Salve, sidus polonorum* was composed for last year's Expo 2000 in Hannover, and commemorates the Polish bishop Wojciech (aka St Adalbert), martyred in 997AD and now the patron saint of Bohemia. Characteristically, Górecki's music ranges from reflection to ecstasy, with telling moments of dissonance and surprise.

György Ligeti (b. 1923)

Étude XVIII

UK premiere • PCM 5

Ligeti's *Études* for solo piano are true studies – he composed the first in 1985 to conquer a compositional impasse brought on by the problems of composing a commissioned piano concerto. The problems surmounted, he finished the concerto in 1988 and continued to write more of these miniatures, completing a *deuxième livre* in 1994 and starting a *troisième livre* the following year. *Étude XVII* was a BBC commission for *Sounding the Century*. Never afraid to reinvent himself, Ligeti's recent works have explored different tempering and tuning systems, as heard when he brought his *Hamburg Concerto* and Hungarian songs, *Sippal, Dobbal, Nádihegedüvel*, to the South Bank earlier this year. The piano, though, is equally tempered – so these studies represent a parallel strand to Ligeti's explorations.

Stuart MacRae (b. 1976)

Violin Concerto

World premiere • Prom 14

Stuart MacRae first came to attention as a finalist in the 1996 Lloyd's Bank Young Composers Workshop, and is now Composer-in-Association with the BBC Scottish Symphony Orchestra. His debut work for the BBC Proms is a violin concerto for Tasmin Little. Describing the work as 'an ensemble of ideas rather than a two-way conversation or argument', MacRae prefers not to think of violin and orchestra as two characters in opposition. 'I wanted to give each of them several characters, some of which are shared, others specific. The result of this is that there is no clear or fixed relationship between the two, but rather a flexibility allowing each to come into focus at different times.'

Christopher Rouse (b. 1949)

Seeing

European premiere • Prom 6

A broad-ranging musician, Christopher Rouse followed the traditional 'classical' route through conservatory and university, but maintained a parallel interest in popular music – and has even taught an academic course on rock. Having made his mark with a pair of enthusiastically-received symphonies, he turned to concertos, of which he has now written several, including *Der gerettete Alberich* for the percussionist Evelyn Glennie and *Concert de Gaudí* for the guitarist Sharon Isbin. *Seeing* is a concerto for piano, composed for Emanuel Ax and premiered in New York in 1999 under Leonard Slatkin. Rouse calls the work a meditation on madness, and claims as inspiration the tragic stories of Robert Schumann and the late Skip Spence, a rock guitarist and songwriter afflicted with schizophrenia.

Esa-Pekka Salonen (b. 1958)

Foreign Bodies

UK premiere • Prom 34

Esa-Pekka Salonen is probably better known as a dynamic young Finnish conductor than as a dynamic young Finnish composer – but the man who gave his name as Mozart when sitting the Sibelius Academy's entrance exam considers himself a composer first. 'Basically the piece is a synthesis of all the thinking and new ideas I developed during my sabbatical year in 2000,' he explains. 'The title refers to the fact that my 10 years in California have helped me to think in a simpler, more direct way than before. I love Los Angeles – and yet I feel foreign, a misplaced, shy northerner amidst extrovert and confident Californians. This polarity is quite inspiring – in my worst moments I feel like some kind of middle-aged Tonio Kröger!"

Sir John Tavener (b. 1944)

Song of the Cosmos

World premiere • Prom 20

Spatially distributed orchestras, banks of eastern percussion, a soprano representing Sofia, the ecstatic female part of the Godhead – it could only be the latest work from Sir John Tavener, following on from the restful serenity and ground-shaking climaxes of *Fall and Resurrection*, premiered at St Paul's Cathedral last year. Commissioned to celebrate the 125th anniversary of the Bach Choir, *Song of the Cosmos* once again gives a starring role to Tavener's muse, Patricia Rozario (pictured with the composer, *below*). Tavener describes the work as 'a sort of crescendo, leading to the incomplete final section which denotes the summit of man's reasoning and understanding. We can go no further.'

Augusta Read Thomas (b. 1964)

Aurora

UK premiere • Prom 65

Aurora was composed for Daniel Barenboim to conduct from the keyboard – thus bringing his dream of directing the Mozart concertos from the piano into the 21st century. Yet Augusta Read Thomas is adamant that it isn't a concerto. 'I'm fairly terrified of writing for piano, because I think it's an extremely difficult thing to do. You either fall into these Rakhmaninov-isms, or Chopin-isms, or you do an obligatory fugue.' *Aurora*, though, is a work that unfolds kaleidoscopically, almost organically. Calling on Barenboim's broad range of pianistic resources, Thomas says, 'It's almost as if I'm asking him to caress the piano, as opposed to playing it.'

APPLAUSE?

A DONATION TO THE MUSICIANS BENEVOLENT FUND CAN DO SO MUCH TO HELP NEEDY MUSICIANS AND THOSE IN CLOSELY RELATED OCCUPATIONS — FOR WHOM ACCIDENT OR ILLNESS CAN LEAD TO DESPAIR AND EVEN SILENCE.

PLEASE SEND US A DONATION AND CONSIDER REMEMBERING US IN YOUR WILL.

MUSICIANS BENEVOLENT FUND, 16 OGLE STREET, LONDON W1P 8JB.
TEL: 020 7636 4481 FAX: 020 7637 4307
EMAIL: info@mbf.org.uk WEBSITE: http://www.mbf.org.uk
REGISTERED CHARITY NO. 228089.

John Howard Hotel

£110 per double/twin

Why not make your visit to the "Proms" a night to remember with an overnight stay at this elegant and luxurious hotel on the doorstep of the Royal Albert Hall.

The rate per night is inclusive of VAT, Service and Full Buffet Breakfast.

**4 QUEENS GATE
LONDON SW7 5EH
TEL: 020 7808 8400
FAX: 020 7808 8402**

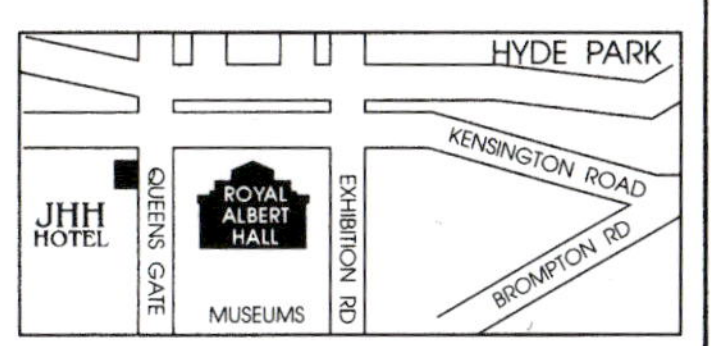

INTERNATIONAL CONCERT SERIES 2001 - 2002

ALFRED BRENDEL   TRULS MØRK

NEEME JÄRVI   MIKHAIL PLETNEV

VALERY GERGIEV   JAMES GALWAY

RADU LUPU   VLADIMIR ASHKENAZY

ESA-PEKKA SALONEN   SIR COLIN DAVIS

SIR ROGER NORRINGTON   LEONARD SLATKIN

FOR YOUR FREE BROCHURE: BOX OFFICE TEL 01256 844244   TICKETFAX 01256 366900   WWW.THEANVIL.ORG.UK

THE ANVIL
BASINGSTOKE

"DESIGNED WITHOUT COMPROMISE AS AN IDEAL CONCERT HALL" THE OBSERVER   M3 J6 OR BY RAIL: BASINGSTOKE

BBC *Symphony* Orchestra

LEONARD SLATKIN CHIEF CONDUCTOR

After the success of their first season together, Leonard Slatkin and the BBC Symphony Orchestra are set to go from strength to strength in 2001-2002. As well as drawing upon the rich legacy of 20th century music, the Orchestra will continue to showcase 21st century composers with performances of new pieces by Mark-Anthony Turnage, John Adams, Steve Martland, Kevin Volans and Brian Elias.

As well as welcoming back Conductor Laureate Sir Andrew Davis, guest artists include Donald Runnicles, Jiří Bělohlávek, Neeme Järvi, Evgeny Svetlanov, Jukka-Pekka Saraste, Jean-Yves Thibaudet, Michelle de Young and Kim Kashkashian.

Season Highlights

- **Stravinsky's** opera-oratorio *Oedipus Rex* (6 October)

- **Britten's** War Requiem (10 November)

- Composer Portraits of **Philip Glass** (6 December) and **Morton Feldman** (1 February)

- **John Adams Weekend**. An opportunity to focus on the works of this composer, including the UK premiere of *The Death of Klinghoffer*, with Adams conducting and talking about his work (18-20 January)

- The complete **Bernstein Symphonies**, conducted by Leonard Slatkin (21 & 23 February)

- **Janáček's** opera *Osud*, conducted by Jiří Bělohlávek (30 May)

Leonard Slatkin lifts his baton for the First Night of the Proms on 20 July. Between then and the Last Night, the BBC Symphony Orchestra will be appearing in fourteen Proms.

There's far too much to tell you about here, so call 020 7765 2549 to receive a copy of our season brochure and to join the free mailing list, or register at www.bbc.co.uk/orchestras/so

Box Office
020 7638 8891 (bkg fee)
www.barbican.org.uk

barbican

BBC RADIO 3

Leonard Slatkin © Keith Saunders

'American conductor Leonard Slatkin
has been appointed Andrew Davis's
successor at the BBC Symphony
Orchestra … I can't think of a better
man for the job. Slatkin is articulate,
intelligent, unstuffy and good with
audiences. He's also a superb musician.'
Michael White (*The Independent on Sunday*,
14 November 1999)

With all flags flying

Edward Seckerson profiles Leonard Slatkin, the BBC Symphony Orchestra's new Chief Conductor, as he prepares to launch into his first Proms season

Uncle Sam, as Leonard Slatkin will tell you, is not one to bear a grudge, but now that he has officially moved in with Auntie, the American maestro would like to set the record straight. Better yet, get even.

I think it's safe to say that Slatkin's first Proms season with the BBC Symphony Orchestra will end more auspiciously than the 'special relationship' between our two nations began. And lest we forget *how* it began, Slatkin plans to – how to put this? – jog our memories. So, on this year's Last Night, he'll be ringing *The Liberty Bell* in the land of hope and glory. Monty Python might characterise that as John Philip Sousa putting the boot into Elgar, though I doubt that even the Pythons would think it quite so hilarious that the Yanks should have pinched Britain's National Anthem and called it *America*. 'Spoils of war,' says Slatkin. It could have been worse. Charles Ives could have written a piece called *Variations on 'Jerusalem'*.

Looking at Slatkin's Last Night programme – indeed his whole first season – the works he's chosen tell you a great deal about who he is. Last Night jokes aside, his first season was bound to

embrace his two great loves – British and American music – and so it does, with even-handed diplomacy. But a deeper unity is reflected in the programming.

On opening night (Prom 1), John Adams's *Harmonium* – a work whose title alone reads like a resounding endorsement of Slatkin's first season – unites English and American visionaries, John Donne and Emily Dickinson, in piloting Adams's starship toward eternity. And with Vaughan Williams's *Serenade to Music*, Shakespeare's balmy Belmont and Dickinson's 'Wild Nights' (the last of *Harmonium*'s three movements) find kinship in 'touches of sweet harmony'. Later in the season, Vaughan Williams's *A Sea Symphony* (Prom 67) finds Walt Whitman adrift on 'the limitless heaving breast' that is the sea itself – another neat metaphor for that which divides (and also unites) the old country and the new world.

Nor is it any accident that another of the First Night works – the Overture to Britten's American 'musical' *Paul Bunyan* – looks forward to the Last Night. What better way, after all, to celebrate the wackier by-products of Anglo-American cross-fertilisation than Constant

Lambert's jazz-inflected *The Rio Grande* – a work that brings South America closer to South Kensington than you might ever have imagined.

All this plus a late-night paean to jazz and jazzers (Prom 45), starting with Duke Ellington's *Harlem* (some indication of the anticipated temperature levels) and culminating in the Piano Concerto of Michel Camilo – Latin America's answer to Oscar Peterson – a score so black with notes that Slatkin, upon receiving it, was moved to ask: 'Michel, are you really going to play everything you wrote down?' To which came the reply: 'Oh, I'll add the other stuff later.'

So, enormous stylistic diversity. It's always been Slatkin's watchword. But that was the world, the environment, into which he was born: Hollywood, the Forties. The City of Angels was also the city of immigrants.

ABOVE
Monty Python puts the boot in – cue the sound of Sousa's *Liberty Bell* march (named after the bell that rang out America's declaration of independence in July 1776)

LEFT
Leonard Slatkin beside the Albert Memorial

RIGHT
Hot out of Harlem: Duke Ellington

Prom 42 – with its roll-call of Copland, Barber, Bernstein, Stravinsky and Rakhmaninov (*Rhapsody on a Theme of Paganini* – one of Slatkin's 'perfect' pieces) – reflects that. This Prom is for them: the musical sons of immigrants. All their journeys began in Eastern Europe but not all passed through Ellis Island. There were those, like Slatkin's father Felix, who went directly West.

The movie business provided a handsome living for top-flight musicians. The Slatkins flourished. Felix and his wife Eleanor Aller went to Warner Brothers, Felix later defecting to 20th Century Fox. Chances are that any violin, cello or piano solo of that period would go to a Slatkin. Bernard Herrmann's score for *The Day the Earth Stood Still* featured the first use of electric violin – that was Felix. The Bette Davis/Claude Rains/ Paul Henreid movie *Deception* featured a specially composed Cello Concerto by

Erich Korngold – that was Eleanor. *The Beast with Five Fingers*, starring Peter Lorre – that was Uncle Victor. And guess who provided the whizzbang piano glissando pay-off for Warner's *Looney Tunes*. Uncle Victor again. Oh, and I nearly forgot: Felix and Eleanor also founded the Hollywood String Quartet. The name was criticised. You can't be serious, said some. But they were. Serious enough to attract a succession of legendary names *chez* Slatkin: Stravinsky, Schoenberg, Walton, Villa-Lobos, Sinatra. Yes, Sinatra. So you can see where the diversity comes from.

Jump-cut to the Juilliard School in New York, where Leonard's teacher Jean Morel (his French connection – hence the Ravel and Canteloube on the Last Night) gave him his first hot tip: 'Remember, when you stand in front of an orchestra of 100 players, there are probably about 80 who think they can conduct better than you can, and 20 who can!'

It was good advice. André Previn once said to Slatkin: 'Man, your beat's so clear Helen Keller could follow it!' So Slatkin gives the lie to the popular misconception that a clear beat and a super-efficient rehearsal technique somehow signify superficiality. Is the reverse true, he asks? Do woolly techniques and wordy rehearsals automatically signify inspiration?

Slatkin comes to the BBC with a fantastic track record for orchestra-building. His 16-plus years as Music Director of the St Louis Symphony took America's second oldest orchestra from

good-but-anonymous, from the second or third division, into the premier league (that's baseball not soccer, of course). In Washington, where he currently resides, the National Symphony (and it, too, is headed up the American league table) reflects the national character. Slatkin recalls a time when orchestras were known as much for *what* they played as *how* they played it. Identity is a big thing for him. He wants the BBC Symphony Orchestra to take pride in its national identity and, in so doing, to consolidate its international profile through the music of its own country. When they tour the USA in a couple of years' time, the programmes will be all-British. And if that sounds a little too much like jingoism, remember that Slatkin is too passionate an advocate of too many things ever to paint himself into any one corner.

In the meantime, there are those old scores to settle. We eagerly await his first Last Night speech. Or should that be 'commentary'? Uncle Sam as master of ceremonies, maybe, with Auntie all ears?

One thing is certain, though. The home crowd had better get used to seeing stars and stripes.

A group of European refugees arrive at Ellis Island in 1926. Between 1892 and 1954, over 12 million immigrants to the USA passed through this island portal erected in the shadow of the Statue of Liberty

The Hollywood String Quartet, founded by Leonard Slatkin's parents, Felix and Eleanor

Leonard Slatkin (left) / AKG Photo London (above)

84

The BBC Symphony Orchestra

Founded in 1930, the BBC Symphony Orchestra played for every Prom throughout its first decade. In these days of more adequate rehearsal and preparation, the BBC SO is still the linchpin of the season, giving more concerts than any other orchestra, but now shares the bill with its fellow BBC orchestras and visiting groups from home and abroad. This season, in addition to six concerts with Leonard Slatkin, it will be playing under six other conductors:

Sir Andrew Davis Proms 12 and 17

Having stepped down last year after 11 seasons as the BBC SO's Chief Conductor, Sir Andrew returns twice to the Proms in 2001 as the orchestra's first ever Conductor Laureate.

Evgeny Svetlanov Prom 25

Former Principal Conductor of the USSR (later Russian) State Symphony Orchestra, the Moscow-born Svetlanov returns to conduct a mainly Russian programme.

David Robertson Prom 30

Trained at London's Royal Academy of Music, the California-born Robertson became Music Director of the Orchestre National de Lyon at the start of this season. A former MD of the Ensemble InterContemporain in Paris, he returns to the Proms to conduct both the UK premiere of Pierre Boulez's latest *Notation* and the world premiere of Tobias Picker's Cello Concerto.

Esa-Pekka Salonen Prom 36

An increasingly prominent composer with a premiere of his own in the season (see *Prom 34*), the Finnish-born Music Director of the Los Angeles Philharmonic returns to the Proms to conduct a concert of music by exiled composers, including the Ligeti Requiem memorably used on the soundtrack of Stanley Kubrick's *2001: A Space Odyssey*.

Pierre Boulez Prom 51

One of the most influential composers of the post-war avant-garde, with a major UK premiere of his own in the season (see *Prom 30*), this former Chief Conductor of the BBC SO returns to the Proms to conduct the orchestra in key 20th-century works by Bartók, Schoenberg and himself.

John Adams Prom 62

One of this year's featured composers (see *page 34*), Adams makes his conducting debut with the BBC SO in a concert pairing three French pieces with the London premiere of a big orchestral work of his own.

BELOW
Sir Andrew Davis in action at last year's Last Night, his farewell concert as Chief Conductor of the BBC SO

Evgeny Svetlanov

David Robertson

Esa-Pekka Salonen

Pierre Boulez

John Adams

NDR Symphony Orchestra, Hamburg
Prom 46

Recruited amid the rubble of wartorn Germany, Hamburg's 'North German Radio Symphony Orchestra' gave its first concert under Hans Schmidt-Isserstedt in November 1945, when it was hailed in the American press as 'the old world's youngest major orchestra'. Alongside the great classical and romantic works, the NDR SO also specialises in contemporary music; over the years, it has premiered pieces by Henze, Ligeti, Schoenberg, Stravinsky, Zimmermann and Krzysztof Penderecki, who is also its Permanent Guest Conductor. Following Schmidt-Isserstedt, Chief Conductors have included Moshe Atzmon, Klaus Tennstedt, Sir John Eliot Gardiner (1991–4) and Herbert Blomstedt (1996–8). Since 1998 its Chief Conductor has been Christoph Eschenbach. For its Proms debut, however, the NDR SO is conducted by Günter Wand, its Chief Conductor from 1982 until 1990, and currently its Honorary Chief Conductor for Life. Together, they have recorded all the symphonies of Beethoven and Brahms, as well as the major symphonies of Bruckner, whose works Wand has memorably

Boston Symphony Orchestra
Proms 47 and 48

Fresh from a season celebrating the centenary of Symphony Hall, its Boston base, the BSO returns to the Proms for the first time since 1991 with a pair of concerts under Bernard Haitink marking the 50th anniversary of the death of Serge Koussevitzky, the legendary Russian-Jewish conductor who took over the Boston SO from Pierre Monteux in 1924 and went on to conduct it for the next quarter of a century.

A dedicated champion of contemporary music, Koussevitzky had founded his own music publishing house in Russia in 1909, while still in his 30s, publishing new works by Skryabin, Stravinsky, Prokofiev, Medtner and Rakhmaninov. On leaving the USSR in 1920, he moved first to Berlin, then to Paris, where he commissioned Ravel's popular orchestration of Musorgsky's *Pictures at an Exhibition*. During his 25 years in Boston, Koussevitzky premiered 99 works, including both Martinů's Sixth Symphony and Stravinsky's *Symphony of Psalms*, two of the works which Bernard Haitink and the Boston orchestra are bringing to this year's Proms.

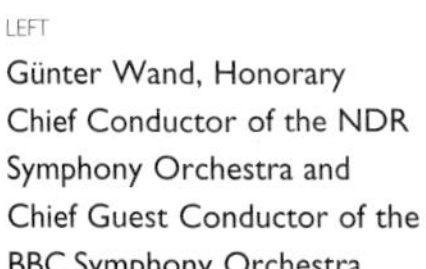

NHK Symphony Orchestra, Tokyo
Prom 49

Japan's oldest professional orchestra was founded as the New Symphony Orchestra in 1926, renamed the Japan Symphony Orchestra in 1942, and only adopted its current name in 1951, although its concerts had been broadcast by its new paymasters, the NHK – Nippon Hoso Kyokai, Japan's public-service counterpart of the BBC – ever since 1936. Over the years, the NHK SO has benefited from inviting a series of distinguished Western guest conductors to work with it, including Karajan, Martinon, Ansermet and Wolfgang Sawallisch, who remains its Honorary Conductor Laureate, and more recently Horst Stein, Herbert Blomstedt, Zubin Mehta and Valery Gergiev. The appointment of Charles Dutoit as Principal Conductor in 1996, coinciding with the orchestra's 70th-birthday celebrations, is widely seen as marking a turning-point in the NHK SO's history. And it is with Dutoit (now Music Director) that they return to the Proms for the first time since making their debut under their then Permanent Conductor, Hiroyuki Iwaki, in 1972.

Leipzig Gewandhaus Orchestra
Proms 53 and 54

The oldest civic orchestra in Germany, the Leipzig Gewandhaus was founded in 1743 by a circle of music-loving citizens. As the Grand Concert Orchestra, its activities originally took place in The Three Swans inn, before transferring in 1781 to a new concert hall built within the former drapers' hall from which it now derives both its name and motto – *Res severa verum gaudium* ('Real pleasure is a serious matter') – though its current home is in fact a modern replacement, opened in 1981, for a second, larger 'Gewandhaus' built in 1884 but destroyed in the war. The orchestra first began to acquire an international reputation when Mendelssohn became its Kapellmeister in 1835. His successors have included such famous names as Arthur Nikisch and Bruno Walter (removed from his post by the Nazis in 1933). The orchestra first visited the Proms in 1988 with Kurt Masur, its Music Director from 1970 to 1996, when he was elected its first Conductor Emeritus. He was succeeded in 1998 by Herbert Blomstedt, who brings the orchestra back to the Proms for its fourth visit – with some Mendelssohn, as ever, on the menu.

Chicago Symphony Orchestra
Proms 63 and 65

Founded in 1891, the Chicago Symphony only really came into its own when the Hungarian-born conductor Fritz Reiner took it in hand in 1953 and turned it into what Stravinsky called 'the most precise and flexible orchestra in the world'. Reiner was followed in 1963 by Jean Martinon, and in 1969 by the late Georg Solti, who brought the orchestra to the Proms for the first time in 1978, returning with it in 1981 and 1989. Two years later he was succeeded as Music Director by Daniel Barenboim, who recalled his first hearing of the orchestra as a teenager – playing Strauss's *Ein Heldenleben* under Reiner in 1958 – as 'an artistic revelation', and hailed his own appointment as 'the dream I never dared to dream'. He first brought the CSO to the Proms in 1996, the first time he had conducted at these concerts since 1981. This year, Augusta Read Thomas's *Aurora* gives him a chance to shine in the twin roles of conductor and pianist.

Orchestre de Paris
Proms 68 and 70

Founded in 1967 by France's then Minister of Culture, André Malraux, the Orchestre de Paris is directly descended from one of the oldest orchestras in the world, the Société des Concerts du Conservatoire, itself founded in 1828. Charles Münch, the orchestra's first Music Director, was succeeded in turn by Herbert von Karajan, Georg Solti and Daniel Barenboim, with whom the orchestra made its Proms debut in 1981. It has returned twice since then: under Pierre Boulez in 1985, and under Semyon Bychkov, Barenboim's successor, in 1991. Bychkov was followed in 1998 by Christoph von Dohnányi, from whom Christoph Eschenbach took over last September. Originally known as a pianist, Eschenbach was recently appointed Music Director in Philadelphia, to add to his existing roles in Paris and Hamburg.

'I have always felt, in our rehearsals, as if we're all members of the same family … I think we can be happy together'
Christoph Eschenbach

Other visiting orchestras at Proms 2001

SWR Stuttgart RSO/Sir Roger Norrington	*Prom 4*
European Union Youth Orchestra/Sir Colin Davis	*Prom 22*
Ulster Orchestra/Dmitri Sitkovetsky	*Prom 23*
Austro-Hungarian Haydn Orchestra/Adám Fischer	*Prom 26*
Gothenburg SO/Neeme Järvi	*Prom 27*
Finnish Radio SO/Jukka-Pekka Saraste	*Prom 34*
St Petersburg PO/Yuri Temirkanov	*Prom 43*
Kirov Orchestra/Valery Gergiev	*Prom 50*
Czech PO/Vladimir Ashkenazy	*Proms 58 and 60*

How to Book

• Priority Booking

By post and fax – opens on Monday 21 May

To take advantage of the priority booking period – and enjoy your best chance of securing the seats you want – use the exclusive easy-fax Booking Form, facing page 122. Note that all postal and fax bookings received before 21 May will be treated as if they had arrived on that date.

Postal address: BBC Proms, Box Office, Royal Albert Hall, Kensington Gore, London SW7 2AP

Fax number: 020 7581 9311

• General Booking

In person or by telephone – opens on Friday 15 June

The Box Office is located at Door 9 of the Royal Albert Hall and is open 9.00am–9.00pm daily. Note that no booking fee applies to tickets bought in person at the Hall.

Telephone number: 020 7589 8212

• How to Prom

Don't book, just turn up and stand.
Up to 1,000 standing places in the Arena and Gallery are available at the door for every Prom (except the Last Night). Proms Season Tickets (covering all or half the season) are bookable in advance (by post or in person).
See page 118 for details.

• Special Offers

See pages 112–13 for details.

• The Last Night of the Proms

Because of the high demand for tickets to the Last Night, special booking arrangements apply.
See page 119 for details.

Last Night Ballot
Exclusive to readers of the *BBC Proms 2001 Guide*
Your chance to enter this year's Last Night Ballot and apply for tickets to the Last Night. See page 119.

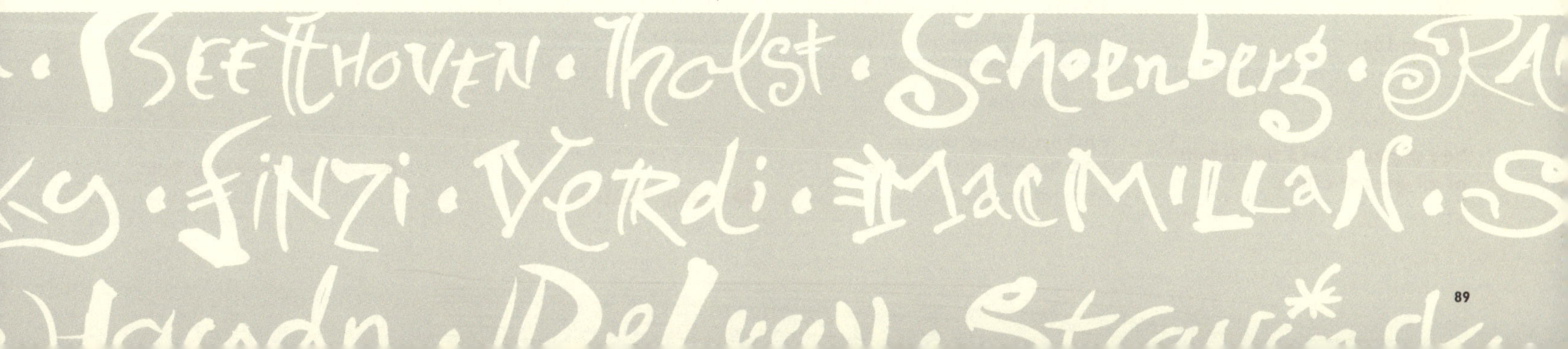

Explore the Proms with these special offers

Look out for the following symbols above selected concerts and save money!

Proms Explorer

Spoilt for choice? Let us help you decide which concerts to go to – and save you money.

Same Day Savers

Go to an evening concert, stay on for the Late Night Prom and save £2.00 per person.

Premieres

Enjoy discounts on concerts which contain premieres. Look for the sign.

Group Bookings

Go in a group of 10 or more and save 10% on your booking.

Under-16s

Go half-price if you're under 16.

See pages 112–13 for details of all special offers

PROM 1

Friday 20 July
7.30pm – c9.30pm
Price Code **B**

Colin Matthews
Fanfare   2'
BBC commission: world premiere

Britten, orch. Colin Matthews
Overture 'Paul Bunyan'   5'

Vaughan Williams
Serenade to Music   15'

Elgar
Cello Concerto in E minor   28'

interval

John Adams
Harmonium   32'

**Orla Boylan, Sarah Fox,
Gweneth-Ann Jeffers,
Sally Matthews** *sopranos*

**Sally Bruce-Payne, Anna Burford,
Sarah Connolly, Emma Curtis**
mezzo-sopranos

**Alfred Boe, Wynne Evans,
Gwyn Hughes Jones, Rhys Meirion**
tenors

Leigh Melrose, Håkan Vramsmo
baritones

**Jonathan Lemalu,
James Rutherford** *basses*

Guy Johnston *cello*

BBC Symphony Chorus
BBC Symphony Orchestra
Leonard Slatkin *conductor*

Britain meets America in this year's opening concert, which includes one of the greatest popular concertos and a contemporary choral classic. John Adams's *Harmonium* brings together texts by the Englishman John Donne and the American Emily Dickinson – and John Adams returns later in the season both as composer and conductor (see Proms 62 and 73). The original overture to Benjamin Britten's early operetta, written during his self-imposed wartime exile in the New World, is heard for the first time at the Proms, in Colin Matthews's scoring. Matthews himself provides the opening flourish to this year's season with a specially commissioned fanfare (*see page 72*). A host of leading young singers perform Vaughan Williams's *Serenade to Music* (written for Henry Wood) to welcome Leonard Slatkin to his first Proms season as the BBC Symphony Orchestra's new Chief Conductor (*see pages 82–84*). Guy Johnston, who memorably won BBC Young Musicians 2000, performs Elgar's evergreen Cello Concerto.

This concert will be broadcast on BBC Television

6.00pm Poetry Prom
See page 131

PROM 2

Saturday 21 July
7.30pm – c10.00pm
Price Code **B**

Handel
L'Allegro, il Penseroso ed
il Moderato   114'

Tristan Hambleton *treble*
Sophie Daneman *soprano*
Anna-Maria Panzarella *soprano*
Paul Agnew *tenor*
Anton Scharinger *bass*

Les Arts Florissants
William Christie *conductor*

Handel's glorious elegy to the English countryside and urban bustle brings together texts by John Milton and Charles Jennens (the compiler of the texts for *Messiah*), setting them to the most ravishing music in the pastoral tradition. France's leading Baroque ensemble Les Arts Florissants returns with its inspirational American-born conductor, William Christie, after their past Proms successes with Handel's *Semele* and Rameau's *Zoroastre*.

There will be one interval

6.00pm Pre-Prom Talk
William Christie talks to
Nicholas Kenyon, Director of the Proms

PROM 3
Sunday 22 July
7.30pm – *c*10.00pm
Price Code **B**

Verdi
Overture 'Nabucco' — 7'
Il trovatore – Act 1 scene 2 — 18'
Don Carlos – Act 4 scene 1 — 37'

interval

Verdi
Aida – Prelude to Act 1 — 5'
Aida – Act 2 (complete) — 41'

Veronica Villarroel *soprano*
Dolora Zajick *mezzo-soprano*
Leah-Marian Jones *mezzo-soprano*
Carlo Ventre *tenor*
Vassily Gerello *baritone*
Alexander Anisimov *bass*
Alastair Miles *bass*

Hallé Choir
Leeds Festival Chorus
London Symphony Chorus
Hallé Orchestra
Mark Elder *conductor*

A century after the death of Verdi, one of his leading British exponents, in his first season at the helm of the Hallé, conducts a collection of key scenes from his major operas contrasting private tragedy with public pomp and ceremony, and touching upon this year's theme of the music of exile. (See 'Verdi', pages 42–45.)

💬 **3.30pm Verdi Study Event**
Chaired by Roger Parker with Pierluigi Petrobelli. See *pages 131–4*

PROM 4
Monday 23 July
7.30pm – *c*9.40pm
Price Code **A**

Weber
Overture 'Oberon' — 9'

Vaughan Williams
Symphony No. 3, 'Pastoral' — 36'

interval

Schubert
Symphony No. 9, 'Great C major' — 53'

Sibylla Rubens *soprano*

SWR Stuttgart Radio Symphony Orchestra
Sir Roger Norrington *conductor*

Sir Roger Norrington, renowned as a leading light in the historical performance movement, brings the SWR Stuttgart RSO on its first visit to the Proms. Echoes of nature suffuse the overture to Weber's fairyland opera, while shadows of war haunt Vaughan Williams's 'Pastoral' Symphony. Schubert's monumental final symphony – which he never heard performed – is a central work of the Classical repertoire that Norrington has done so much to revivify over the past three decades.

🎵 **1.00pm Proms Chamber Music**
See *pages 110–11*

PROM 5
Tuesday 24 July
7.30pm – *c*9.45pm
Price Code **A**

Schnittke
Moz-Art à la Haydn — 12'

Tchaikovsky/Raskatov
Seasons Digest — 16'
UK premiere

Liszt/Dreznin
Concert Fantasy for violin and strings after 'Après une lecture du Dante' — 17'
UK premiere

interval

Schubert
String Quintet in C major
(arr. Kremerata Baltica) — 45'

Kremerata Baltica
Eva Bindere *violin*
Gidon Kremer *violin/director*

Gidon Kremer returns to London following his highly praised appearances at the Barbican in the BBC Symphony Orchestra's Schnittke Weekend in January. He and his young virtuoso ensemble present familiar music clad in unfamiliar colours, from Schnittke's witty reconstruction of fragments by Mozart to an expansion for string orchestra of Schubert's heart-rending Quintet – by way of a fantasy on one of Liszt's best-known piano works and a digest from Tchaikovsky's seasonal cycle for piano.

PROM 6
Wednesday 25 July
7.00pm – *c*9.25pm
Price Code **A**

NOTE TIME

Mahler, arr. Britten
What the Wild Flowers Tell Me — 10'

Christopher Rouse
Seeing — 30'
European premiere

interval

Mahler
Symphony No. 5 — 71'

Emanuel Ax *piano*

BBC Symphony Orchestra
Leonard Slatkin *conductor*

During Benjamin Britten's wartime stay in America, he prepared *What the Wild Flowers Tell Me* from Mahler's Third Symphony to bring the music of this then-unfamiliar composer to a wider US audience. Mahler's Fifth Symphony remains one of the best-loved of his works, especially since its use in Luchino Visconti's film of Thomas Mann's *Death in Venice*. Emanuel Ax gives the European premiere of a recent concerto by Christopher Rouse, a 'meditation on madness', premiered in America by Ax and Slatkin in 1999 (see *page 76*).

💬 **5.30pm Pre-Prom Talk**
Christopher Rouse and Emanuel Ax in conversation with Rob Cowan

PROM 7 

Wednesday 25 July
10.00pm – c11.30pm
Price Code **D**

LATE NIGHT

Byrd
Mass for Five Voices — 25'

Tallis
Lamentations I — 9'

Bull
Doctor Bull's my selfe — 2'
Gloria tibi Trinitas — 4'
Ut re mi fa sol la — 5'

Ferrabosco I
Lamentations — 8'

Byrd
Ne irascaris, Domine — 9'

Tallis
Spem in alium — 9'

Catherine Ennis organ

The Tallis Scholars
Peter Phillips director

The Tallis Scholars make a belated debut at the Proms with a programme based around the Lamentations of Jeremiah. Byrd's beautiful Mass opens this concert of music by composers who were persecuted for their religious beliefs and forced either to perform their music in private, in the homes of the aristocracy, or, in the case of John Bull, to flee into European exile.

There will be no interval

PROM 8 🅟

Thursday 26 July
7.30pm – c9.35pm
Price Code **A**

Rimsky-Korsakov
Russian Easter Festival Overture — 14'

James MacMillan
Birds of Rhiannon* — c30'
BBC commission: world premiere

interval

Strauss
Ein Heldenleben — 43'

The Sixteen
BBC Philharmonic
James MacMillan conductor*
Vassily Sinaisky conductor

Vassily Sinaisky

The BBC Philharmonic's new Composer/ Conductor, James MacMillan, conducts the orchestra for the first time at the Proms in the world premiere of his new work (see *page 72*). Chief Guest Conductor Vassily Sinaisky, who has been praised for his *Carmen* at English National Opera, takes the podium for Rimsky-Korsakov's popular overture and Richard Strauss's unashamedly egocentric portrait of a hero's life.

♪ **6.00pm Composer Portrait**
James MacMillan. See *page 133*

PROM 9 🅔

Friday 27 July
7.30pm – c9.55pm
Price Code **A**

Rubbra
Symphony No. 4 — 28'

Ravel
Piano Concerto in G major — 22'

interval

Elgar
Symphony No. 2 in E flat major — 55'

Jean-Yves Thibaudet piano

BBC National Orchestra of Wales
Richard Hickox conductor

Richard Hickox, who recently became Principal Conductor of the BBC National Orchestra of Wales, brings the orchestra to the Proms for a pair of concerts of English and French music. Here, an English symphonic classic is prefaced by a centenary performance of a rarely heard Rubbra symphony for which Hickox has a special love and which was itself premiered at the Proms nearly 60 years ago. In between, Proms favourite Jean-Yves Thibaudet performs Ravel's jazz-tinged concerto, one of the works commissioned for the Boston Symphony Orchestra's 50th anniversary by its legendary conductor Serge Koussevitzky, who died 50 years ago.

💬 **6.00pm Pre-Prom Talk**
Richard Hickox talks to Paul Guinery

PROM 10 🔞

Saturday 28 July
11.00am – c1.00pm
Price Code **F**

NOTE TIME

BLUE PETER PROM
'Town and Country'

Simon Thomas presenter
Liz Barker presenter

Daniel Hope violin
David Childs euphonium

BBC Philharmonic
Rumon Gamba conductor

Another opportunity to join *Blue Peter* presenters in a fun-filled musical extravaganza for all the family. This year we celebrate the colours and contrasts of town and country life with some great orchestral favourites, including music from Vivaldi's *The Four Seasons*, Copland's *Appalachian Spring* and Bernstein's *West Side Story*. There's a dash of new music, a sprinkling of gifted young soloists, a chance to make your own musical instrument and perform with the BBC Philharmonic – plus a few things you'll recognise from the Last Night of the Proms and lots of surprises too! Story-teller Taffy Thomas brings a new work created specially for this *Blue Peter* Prom with composer Barry Russell and children from schools in Stockport and Cumbria.

There will be one interval

Tom Bangbala

PROM 11

Saturday 28 July
7.30pm – *c*9.40pm
Price Code **A**

Debussy
Printemps (original version)   16'

Finzi
Cello Concerto   36'

interval

Britten
Spring Symphony   44'

Raphael Wallfisch *cello*

Lillian Watson *soprano*
Pamela Helen Stephen *mezzo-soprano*
Philip Langridge *tenor*

BBC Singers
Southend Boys' Choir
**Boys of Colorado Children's
Chorale**
London Symphony Chorus
BBC National Chorus of Wales
BBC National Orchestra of Wales
Richard Hickox *conductor*

We begin our tribute
to centenary composer
Gerald Finzi with his lyrical
Cello Concerto, first heard
at the Proms in 1956, just
weeks before his death.
Developing the Pastoral theme, Britten's
Spring Symphony, which delves into the
English literary past, is contrasted with
Debussy's French vision of spring.

This concert will be broadcast on BBC Television

PROM 12 Ⓟ

Sunday 29 July
7.30pm – *c*9.50pm
Price Code **A**

Sally Beamish
Knotgrass Elegy   *c*40'
BBC commission: world premiere

interval

Prokofiev
Violin Concerto No. 2   27'

Stravinsky
The Firebird – suite (1945)   30'

Susan Bullock *soprano*
Brian Asawa *counter-tenor*
Christopher Maltman *baritone*
Tommy Smith *saxophone*

James Ehnes *violin*

BBC Symphony Chorus
New London Children's Choir
BBC Symphony Orchestra
Sir Andrew Davis *conductor*

Sir Andrew Davis makes a welcome
return in his new role as the BBC
Symphony Orchestra's Conductor
Laureate, and a brilliant young
Canadian violinist makes his debut.
Sally Beamish's first Proms commission
is a topical contemporary take on this
year's pastoral theme (see *page 71*).

This concert will be broadcast on BBC Television

🔴**6.00pm Pre-Prom Talk**
Sally Beamish talks to Lynne Walker

PROM 13 Ⓖ

Monday 30 July
7.30pm – *c*9.40pm
Price Code **A**

Nielsen
Symphony No. 2,
'The Four Temperaments'   33'

Prokofiev
Piano Concerto No. 1
in D flat major   14'

interval

Vaughan Williams
A London Symphony   46'

Louis Lortie *piano*

BBC Scottish Symphony Orchestra
Osmo Vänskä *conductor*

Osmo Vänskä's triumphant partnership
with the BBC Scottish Symphony
Orchestra continues to go from
strength to strength. They bring
Nielsen's study of the humours to the
Proms for the first time, and follow the
mighty Thames through London in
Vaughan Williams's evocation of our
great capital city.

This concert will be broadcast on BBC Television

🎵**1.00pm Proms Chamber Music**
See pages 110–11

PROM 14 ➔Ⓟ

Tuesday 31 July
7.00pm – *c*9.10pm
Price Code **A**

Berlioz
Overture 'Le corsaire'   8'

Stuart MacRae
Violin Concerto   *c*28'
*Richard Gregson-Williams Memorial Trust
commission: world premiere*

interval

Britten
Les illuminations   23'

Strauss
Also sprach Zarathustra   32'

Tasmin Little *violin*

Inger Dam-Jensen *soprano*

BBC Scottish Symphony Orchestra
Martyn Brabbins *conductor*

Proms 2001 would not be complete
without the Strauss tone-poem that set
the scene for Stanley Kubrick's *2001: A
Space Odyssey*. 25-year-old Stuart
MacRae is the BBC Scottish SO's
Composer-in-Association, and wrote
his Concerto especially for tonight's
soloist (see *page 76*). Britten wrote his
sensuous Rimbaud settings in the USA.

This concert will be broadcast on BBC Television

🔴**5.30pm Pre-Prom Talk**
Stuart MacRae and Richard Stilgoe
in conversation with Edward Blakeman

PROM 15

Tuesday 31 July
10.00pm – c11.30pm
Price Code **D**

LATE NIGHT

Beethoven
Adagio and Allegretto from
'The Creatures of Prometheus'   *8'*

Judith Weir, arr. Parrott
Missa del Cid   *25'*

Haydn
Mass in B flat major, 'Creation'   *45'*

Simon Callow *narrator*
(subject to availability)

Emily Van Evera *soprano*
Deborah Miles-Johnson *mezzo-soprano*
Paul Agnew *tenor*
Christian Hilz *bass*

New London Chamber Choir
London Mozart Players
Andrew Parrott *conductor*

Judith Weir

Haydn's penultimate mass, which bears thematic relationships with his great oratorio, *The Creation*, is performed tonight 200 years after it was composed, as is Beethoven's music from *Prometheus*. Judith Weir's *Missa del Cid*, which was composed for television and is rearranged here for chorus, orchestra and narrator by tonight's conductor, sets texts about Christian Spain's legendary champion in the wars against the Moors.

There will be no interval

PROM 16

Wednesday 1 August
7.30pm – c9.40pm
Price Code **C**

Dvořák
Overture 'Carnival'   *9'*

Brahms
Variations on the St Anthony Chorale   *17'*

Mozart
Exsultate, jubilate   *17'*

interval

Strauss
Don Juan   *17'*
Four Last Songs   *21'*

Renée Fleming *soprano*

Philharmonia Orchestra
Christoph Eschenbach *conductor*

Renée Fleming

Soprano Renée Fleming, who boasts a huge worldwide reputation, makes her long-awaited Proms debut in music by the two composers with whom she is most closely associated – a florid Mozart motet and Strauss's ravishing final songs, which were given their posthumous premiere in the Royal Albert Hall. Christoph Eschenbach, who returns with his own Paris orchestra in Proms 68 and 70, adds orchestral favourites by Strauss, Dvořák and Brahms.

This concert will be broadcast on BBC Television

PROM 17

Thursday 2 August
7.30pm – c9.50pm
Price Code **A**

Schoenberg
Variations for Orchestra, Op. 31   *21'*

Rakhmaninov
Piano Concerto No. 1
in F sharp minor   *27'*

interval

Weill
Royal Palace *(sung in German)*   *50'*

Leif Ove Andsnes *piano*

Janice Watson Dejanira
Stephen Richardson Husband
Ashley Holland Yesterday's Lover
Peter Bronder Tomorrow's Admirer
Timothy Robinson Young Fisherman
Clive Bayley Old Fisherman
Camilla Tilling Off-stage Voice

Apollo Voices
BBC Symphony Orchestra
Sir Andrew Davis *conductor*

The big discovery of last year's BBC Kurt Weill Weekend comes to the Proms (*see page 59*), a brilliant Norwegian pianist makes a welcome return and, 50 years after Schoenberg's death, we offer a chance to re-evaluate some of his finest music (*see pages 50–52*).

This concert will be broadcast on BBC Television

🗨 **6.00pm Pre-Prom Talk**
Geoffrey Chew on *Royal Palace*

PROM 18

Friday 3 August
7.00pm – c9.05pm
Price Code **A**

NOTE TIME

Varèse
Arcana   *18'*

Bernstein
Serenade   *30'*

interval

Bernstein, orch. Brohn
West Side Story – suite   *20'*
UK premiere

Ravel
Boléro   *16'*

Joshua Bell *violin*

BBC Philharmonic
Yan Pascal Tortelier *conductor*

The BBC Philharmonic and its Principal Conductor present two sides of Leonard Bernstein – his musing on Plato's *Symposium*, and a brand-new arrangement of songs from his urban musical *West Side Story*, specially prepared for brilliant American violinist Joshua Bell (*see page 74*). Varèse's *Arcana* was inspired by the occult philosophy of Paracelsus, and the concert closes with Ravel's cataclysmic crescendo.

This concert will be broadcast on BBC Television

🗨 **5.30pm Poetry Prom**
See page 131

Telephone booking opens on Friday 15 June: 020 7589 8212

PROM 19

Friday 3 August
10.00pm – c11.30pm
Price Code **D**

LATE NIGHT

THE LATER PROM
Jools Holland
Julian Joseph
Nitin Sawhney

Jools Holland

A late-night jazz evening bringing together some of the hottest talent on the British jazz scene. Pianist and band-leader Jools Holland is also a familiar face on television, having presented *Later with Jools Holland* live on BBC2 for the past nine years; he's joined here by his Rhythm and Blues Orchestra, a band which, he says, occupies 'the beautiful area between swinging jazz, filthy rock 'n' roll and British R 'n' B'.

Julian Joseph

Pianist, band-leader, composer and improviser, Julian Joseph is also a popular BBC voice, as presenter of Radio 3's weekly *Jazz Legends*. No stranger to classical contexts, with his own jazz series at London's Wigmore Hall, he is joined by his Acoustic Trio. The late-night line-up is completed by the award-winning multicultural fusionist Nitin Sawhney, who made his Proms debut as a composer last year.

Nitin Sawhney

There will be no interval

PROM 20

Saturday 4 August
7.30pm – c9.45pm
Price Code **A**

Sir John Tavener
Song of the Cosmos*   c50'
world premiere

interval

Holst
The Planets   50'

Patricia Rozario soprano
Michael George bass

Bach Choir
Waynflete Singers
BBC Philharmonic
David Hill conductor*
Yan Pascal Tortelier conductor

Holst's magical and mystical evocation of the heavens is prefaced by Sir John Tavener's brand-new meditation on the cosmos, commissioned to celebrate the 125th anniversary of the Bach Choir (see *page 77*).

♪**6.00pm Composer Portrait**
Sir John Tavener. *See page 133*

PROM 21

Sunday 5 August
2.30pm – c4.40pm
Price Code **F**

NOTE TIME

THE 'NATION'S FAVOURITE' PROM

Programme to include

Bruch
Violin Concerto No. 1 in G minor   26'

Tchaikovsky
Letter Scene from 'Eugene Onegin'   14'

Elgar
Enigma Variations   30'

Nadja Salerno-Sonnenberg violin

Elena Prokina soprano

Royal Scottish National Orchestra
Paul Daniel conductor

The brilliant young Music Director of English National Opera conducts two of the most popular classics in the repertoire – as recently voted for in a *Radio Times* poll of the 'Nation's Favourite Music' – plus one of the most poignantly romantic scenes in all Russian opera and a few added surprises, in a Sunday-afternoon concert designed to suit all the family.

There will be one interval

This concert will be broadcast on BBC Television

PROM 22

Sunday 5 August
8.00pm – c10.10pm
Price Code **A**

NOTE TIME

Tchaikovsky
Symphony No. 4 in F minor   43'

interval

Elgar
Symphony No. 1 in A flat major   52'

European Union Youth Orchestra
Sir Colin Davis conductor

Sir Colin Davis

The European Union Youth Orchestra is a regular visitor to the Proms. This year it teams up with Sir Colin Davis, continuing his commitment to making music with young musicians, to perform two masterpieces of the symphonic repertoire.

PROM 23 

Monday 6 August
7.00pm – c9.05pm
Price Code **A**

NOTE TIME

Ian Wilson
Man-o'-War   10'
BBC commission: world premiere

Mozart
Sinfonia concertante in E flat major,
for violin and viola, K364   31'

interval

Arvo Pärt
Fratres, for solo violin, strings
and percussion   10'

Shostakovich
Symphony No. 1 in F minor   33'

Nobuko Imai *viola*

Ulster Orchestra
Dmitri Sitkovetsky *violin/conductor*

The Ulster Orchestra and its violin-playing director bring the music of Arvo Pärt, one of many composers who left the Soviet Union to escape official rebuke. Shostakovich remained in Russia and suffered under Stalin's regime. Ian Wilson is a young Northern Irish composer whose music is attracting increasing attention (see *page 74*).

♪ **1.00pm Proms Chamber Music**
See pages 110–11

💬 **5.30pm Pre-Prom Talk**
Ian Wilson talks to Colin Riley

PROM 24 

Monday 6 August
10.00pm – c11.30pm
Price Code **D**

LATE NIGHT

Handel
Acis and Galatea   90'

Rosemary Joshua Galatea
Toby Spence Acis
James Gilchrist Damon
John Tomlinson Polyphemus

**Chorus of the Academy of
Ancient Music**
Academy of Ancient Music
Paul Goodwin *conductor*

Based on the *Metamorphoses* of Ovid, and with poetic input by both Dryden and Pope, Handel's mythological masque was composed in 1718 for the Duke of Chandos's palace at Cannons in Edgware. Though derived from an earlier Italian work, it now seems a perfect example of English pastoral. It is brought to the Proms by one of the foremost period-instrument bands and a British cast, featuring one of the leading Wotans of our day as the jealous giant Polyphemus.

There will be no interval

PROM 25 

Tuesday 7 August
7.30pm – c9.35pm
Price Code **A**

Dukas
The Sorcerer's Apprentice   12'

Tchaikovsky
Violin Concerto in D major   33'

interval

Lyadov
The Enchanted Lake   7'

Musorgsky, orch. Ravel
Pictures at an Exhibition   30'

Vadim Repin *violin*

BBC Symphony Orchestra
Evgeny Svetlanov *conductor*

A magical evening of sorcery and enchantment is presided over by one of the great Russian conductors. Vadim Repin returns following the success of his Shostakovich First Concerto at last year's Proms. Ravel's popular orchestration of Musorgsky's pictorial piano pieces was one of many works commissioned by Serge Koussevitzky, the legendary pre-war conductor of the Boston Symphony Orchestra, who died 50 years ago (see *page 86*).

PROM 26 

Wednesday 8 August
7.00pm – c9.45pm
Price Code **A**

NOTE TIME

Haydn
The Seasons (*sung in German*)   134'

Susan Gritton *soprano*
John Mark Ainsley *tenor*
Neal Davies *bass*

Wiener Singakademie
**Austro-Hungarian Haydn
Orchestra**
Adám Fischer *conductor*

The second of Haydn's two late oratorios – first performed in 1801 – paints a gloriously varied and programmatic picture of the changing times of the year. It is brought to the Proms by the Austro-Hungarian Haydn Orchestra, who are currently recording all of Haydn's symphonies in the great hall at Eisenstadt, where many of them were first performed.

There will be one interval

💬 **5.30pm Pre-Prom Talk**
David Wyn Jones

Fisher (Fischer)

PROM 27 

Thursday 9 August
7.30pm – c9.35pm
Price Code B

Grieg
Peer Gynt – complete incidental music
(sung/spoken in Norwegian)   95'

with English narration spoken by
Paul Scofield

Barbara Bonney Solveig
Randi Stene Anitra
Bo Skovhus Peer Gynt
Wenche Foss Åse
Sverre Anker Ousdal The Narrator/
Great Boyg/Button Moulder

Joar Skorpen *Hardanger fiddle*

BBC Singers
Gothenburg Symphony Orchestra
Neeme Järvi *conductor*

Paul Scofield

From the Norwegian fjords to the Arabian deserts … Grieg's incidental music has taken on a life of its own beyond the Ibsen play it was composed to enliven. This concert offers a rare chance to hear all Grieg's music for *Peer Gynt* in dramatic context (*see page 60*).

There will be one interval

This concert will be broadcast on BBC Television

6.00pm Pre-Prom Talk
Stephen Johnson

PROM 28 

Friday 10 August
7.30pm – c9.30pm
Price Code A

Poul Ruders
Studium   17'
BBC/Danish National Radio SO
co-commission: UK premiere

Lutosławski
Symphony No. 4   21'

interval

Sibelius
Symphony No. 2 in D major   43'

Safri Duo

BBC Philharmonic
Thomas Dausgaard *conductor*

Thomas Dausgaard makes his Proms debut with Lutosławski's last symphony and Sibelius's second, a work whose epic sense of struggle has long been heard as an expression of Finnish nationalism. Poul Ruders's new double percussion concerto, a joint commission from the BBC and the Danish National Radio Symphony Orchestra, was composed for the brilliant Safri Duo, whose recent foray into the world of dance music has been riding high in the pop charts (*see page 73*).

6.00pm Pre-Prom Talk
Poul Ruders talks to Chris de Souza

PROM 29

Saturday 11 August
7.00pm – c9.10pm
Price Code A

Messiaen
Sortie: Le vent de l'Esprit (Messe de la Pentecôte)
Majesté du Christ demandant sa gloire à son père (L'Ascension)
Les mages; Dieu parmi nous (La nativité du Seigneur)   20'

interval

Messiaen
Turangalîla Symphony   75'

Wayne Marshall *organ*

Pierre-Laurent Aimard *piano*
Cynthia Millar *ondes martenot*

National Youth Orchestra of Great Britain
Sir Andrew Davis *conductor*

Annual visitors to the Proms, the National Youth Orchestra brings Messiaen's ravishing hymn to life, love and the universe (*see page 61*). Multi-talented Wayne Marshall prefaces it with a selection of Messiaen's organ music, just before the Albert Hall instrument closes down for renovation. Pierre-Laurent Aimard, a leading exponent of contemporary piano music, also gives a Proms Chamber Music recital on Monday 20 August (*see pages 110–11*).

This concert will be broadcast on BBC Television

PROM 30

Sunday 12 August
7.30pm – c9.35pm
Price Code A

Ives
Three Places in New England   19'

Pierre Boulez
Notations I–IV & VII   20'
UK premiere of Notation VII

interval

Tobias Picker
Cello Concerto   25'
BBC commission: world premiere

Janáček
Sinfonietta   23'

Paul Watkins *cello*

BBC Symphony Orchestra
David Robertson *conductor*

David Robertson returns to the BBC Symphony Orchestra in a unique mix of 20th-century music including two contrasting premieres: the latest of Pierre Boulez's orchestrations of his early piano *Notations* (*see page 75*), and a commission from one of the most successful young US composers (*see page 73*). The pastoral theme continues with Charles Ives's orchestral impressions of the New England countryside.

6.00pm Pre-Prom Talk
Tobias Picker and Paul Watkins in conversation

PROM 31

Monday 13 August
7.30pm – c9.55pm
Price Code **A**

Britten
Two Portraits   15'

Hindemith
Trauermusik   6'

Shostakovich,
arr. Alexander Tchaikovsky
Sinfonia in B flat minor for viola
and strings, arranged from
String Quartet No. 13   27'

interval

Britten
Lachrymae   15'

Tchaikovsky
Souvenir de Florence   34'

Moscow Soloists
Yuri Bashmet viola/director

Yuri Bashmet returns to the Proms
with his young virtuoso ensemble.
Shostakovich's late quartet has been
specially adapted into a viola concerto,
while Britten's *Two Portraits* are also
new to the Proms. Two laments
by Britten and Hindemith contrast
with Tchaikovsky's sunlit memories
of Florence.

♪ **1.00pm Proms Chamber Music**
See pages 110–11

♪ **6.00pm Composer Portrait**
Esa-Pekka Salonen. See page 133

PROM 32 

Tuesday 14 August
7.00pm – c9.25pm
Price Code **A**

NOTE TIME

THE GREAT ESCAPE
Hollywood's Golden Age

Programme to include

Rózsa Ben-Hur

Korngold The Adventures of Robin
Hood

Steiner Gone with the Wind

Tiomkin High Noon

Waxman A Place in the Sun

Elmer Bernstein The Ten
Commandments; The Magnificent
Seven; The Man with the Golden Arm

John Harle saxophone

BBC Concert Orchestra
Elmer Bernstein conductor

Elmer Bernstein, composer and
conductor of some of the most famous
Hollywood film scores, joins top UK
saxophonist John Harle and the BBC
Concert Orchestra in a sequence of
film music from the golden age of
Hollywood, including scores by five
20th-century European composers
whose flights from fascism ended in
Hollywood (see pages 10–11).

There will be one interval

🔊 **5.30pm Pre-Prom Talk**
Details to be announced

PROM 33 

Tuesday 14 August
10.00pm – c11.30pm
Price Code **D**

LATE NIGHT

AN EVENING OF KLEZMER
& GYPSY MUSIC

LAKATOS
David Krakauer's *Klezmer Madness!*

The music of the diaspora and of the
dispossessed. Traditional melodies of
the Gypsies – eternal exiles wherever
they're found – are given a fresh new
slant by fiddler extraordinaire Roby
Lakatos and his Brussels-based band,
already familiar to London audiences
from their regular appearances at
Ronnie Scott's Jazz Club.

Often dubbed the 'Jewish Jazz', Klezmer
is the celebratory music of the ghetto
and the shtetl, the sound that the
'chosen people' have carried with them
wherever they have been forced to
roam. Led by virtuoso New York
clarinettist David Krakauer, the best-
selling *Klezmer Madness!* gives this old
Yiddish music an ultra-modern twist,
mixing rock, jazz, funk, classical and
avant-garde influences into an ancestral
language whose deep roots lie in the
Romanian folk tradition of the *doina* (or
shepherd's song). Part primal scream
therapy, part self-parody, it's new-wave
klezmer with a vengeance, teetering on
the edge of outrageousness.

There will be no interval

PROM 34

Wednesday 15 August
7.30pm – c9.40pm
Price Code **A**

Esa-Pekka Salonen
Foreign Bodies   c17'
UK premiere

Mahler
Des Knaben Wunderhorn
– selection   25'

interval

Sibelius
Symphony No. 6 in D minor   28'
Symphony No. 7 in C major   21'

Katarina Karnéus mezzo-soprano
Dietrich Henschel baritone

Finnish Radio Symphony Orchestra
Jukka-Pekka Saraste conductor

Jukka-Pekka
Saraste

The latest work from
Esa-Pekka Salonen is
performed for the first
time in this country
(see page 77), alongside
Sibelius's two final
symphonies, in a concert conducted by
their compatriot Jukka-Pekka Saraste,
Chief Conductor of the Finnish RSO.
Swedish mezzo-soprano Katarina
Karnéus and German baritone Dietrich
Henschel join them in a selection from
Mahler's set of songs on German
folk texts.

Michael Mitchell

PROM 35

Thursday 16 August
7.30pm – c10.10pm
Price Code **C**

Beethoven
Fidelio
(*sung in German; semi-staged*) 125'

Glyndebourne Festival Opera

Charlotte Margiono Leonore
Kim Begley Florestan
Lisa Milne Marzellina
Timothy Robinson Jacquino
Steven Page Don Pizarro
Alan Opie Don Fernando
Reinhard Hagen Rocco

The Glyndebourne Chorus
Orchestra of the Age of
Enlightenment
Sir Simon Rattle conductor

Beethoven's only opera, a dramatic
hymn to freedom, liberty and human
loyalty, marks the latest collaboration
between Simon Rattle, Glyndebourne
and the period-instrument Orchestra
of the Age of Enlightenment (*see page
62*). It comes to the Proms in a semi-
staged version based on this summer's
new festival production directed by
Deborah Warner.

There will be one interval

🗨**6.00pm Pre-Prom Talk**
Christopher Hailey

PROM 36 

Friday 17 August
7.30pm – c9.35pm
Price Code **A**

György Ligeti
Requiem 30'

interval

Stravinsky
Violin Concerto 22'

Bartók
Concerto for Orchestra 36'

Caroline Stein soprano
Charlotte Hellekant mezzo-soprano

Thomas Zehetmair violin

London Voices
BBC Symphony Orchestra
Esa-Pekka Salonen conductor

Three composers who
left their homelands to
seek refuge in the West.
Ligeti's Requiem was the
work that first made him
famous when its eerie
and atmospheric vocal clusters were
used in the film *2001: A Space Odyssey*.
Bartók's *Concerto for Orchestra* was one
of the many works commissioned by
Serge Koussevitzky, who died 50 years
ago. The brilliant violinist Thomas
Zehetmair performs Stravinsky's neo-
Bachian concerto.

🗨**6.00pm Poetry Prom**
See page 131

PROM 37

Saturday 18 August
7.00pm – c9.15pm
Price Code **A**

Smetana
Vltava from 'Má vlast' 12'

Dvořák
Slavonic Dances – selection 12'

Rodrigo
Concierto Pastoral 24'

interval

Rodrigo
Concierto de Aranjuez 21'

Johann Strauss II
Voices of Spring – waltz 6'
Express – polka 3'
By the Beautiful, Blue Danube
– waltz 9'

Patrick Gallois flute
Manuel Barrueco guitar

BBC Concert Orchestra
Barry Wordsworth conductor

Joaquín Rodrigo's centenary (*see
page 46*) is celebrated with his famous
Concierto de Aranjuez for guitar and his
less familiar 'Pastoral Concerto' for
flute. The pastoral theme is echoed in
both Smetana's flowing evocation of
the river that runs through Prague and
the Strauss waltz that featured so
memorably in the film *2001*.

PROM 38 

Saturday 18 August
10.00pm – c11.30pm
Price Code **D**

Schütz
Three motets from
Geistliche Chorwerke 9'

Brahms
Fest- und Gedenksprüche 9'
Chorale Prelude and Fugue on
'O Traurigkeit, o Herzeleid' 6'

Henryk Górecki
Salve, sidus polonorum 25'
UK premiere

Stravinsky
Concerto for Two Pianos 20'

Schoenberg
De profundis 4'
Friede auf Erden 8'

Philip Moore &
Simon Crawford-Phillips piano duo

David Goode organ

BBC Symphony Chorus
Percussion ensemble
Stephen Jackson conductor

Choral music from the 17th to the 21st
centuries, including a substantial new
work composed by Henryk Górecki for
Expo 2000 in Hanover (*see page 75*).
Early and late works by Schoenberg
rub shoulders with music by Schütz
and Brahms, and a neo-classical double
concerto by Stravinsky.

There will be no interval

PROM 39

Sunday 19 August
7.30pm – c9.35pm
Price Code **A**

Dvořák
Cello Concerto in B minor — 38'

interval

George Benjamin
Sudden Time — 15'

Sibelius
Symphony No. 5 in E flat major — 32'

Heinrich Schiff cello

City of Birmingham Symphony Orchestra
Sakari Oramo conductor

Developing his successful relationship with the CBSO, Sakari Oramo has performed new work and great classics. Here he brings the Fifth Symphony of his compatriot, Sibelius, and performs George Benjamin's vividly atmospheric *Sudden Time*. The leading Austrian cellist, Heinrich Schiff, is the soloist in one of the best-loved concertos.

5.30pm BBC Proms Lecture
Details to be announced
See page 133

PROM 40 

Monday 20 August
7.00pm – c9.20pm
Price Code **A**

NOTE TIME

Mahler
Todtenfeier — 21'

Schoenberg
Violin Concerto, Op. 36 — 31'

interval

Schoenberg
Notturno for violin and strings — 7'
UK premiere

Brahms
Symphony No. 4 in E minor — 41'

Ernst Kovacic violin

BBC National Orchestra of Wales
Joseph Swensen conductor

Schoenberg's Violin Concerto is contrasted with a much earlier short work for violin and orchestra, which has recently been discovered and identified. Brahms and Mahler are both composers who exerted important influences on Schoenberg; *Todtenfeier* ('Funeral Rites') is an early version of the first movement of Mahler's 'Resurrection' Symphony.

♪ **1.00pm Proms Chamber Music**
See pages 110–11

5.30pm Pre-Prom Talk
Christopher Hailey on Schoenberg

PROM 41 

Monday 20 August
10.00pm – c11.40pm
Price Code **D**

LATE NIGHT

Bach, arr. Stravinsky
Chorale Variations on 'Vom Himmel hoch' — 12'

Stravinsky
Canticum sacrum — 17'

Xenakis
Polla ta dhina — 6'

Kenneth Hesketh
Circling Canopy of Light — 25'

Hans Werner Henze
Symphony No. 1 — 18'

Christopher Gillett tenor
David Wilson-Johnson bass-baritone

London Sinfonietta Chorus
London Sinfonietta
Oliver Knussen conductor

Stravinsky orchestrated Bach's Chorale Variations to form a companion piece to his own *Canticum sacrum*. Young British composer Kenneth Hesketh is a protégé of Hans Werner Henze, whose 75th birthday is marked with a performance of his youthful First Symphony. Iannis Xenakis, who died in February, is commemorated with the performance of one of his early choral works.

There will be no interval

PROM 42

Tuesday 21 August
7.30pm – c9.50pm
Price Code **A**

Copland
El salón México — 11'

Barber
Adagio for Strings — 9'

Bernstein
Symphony No. 1, 'Jeremiah' — 25'

interval

Rakhmaninov
Rhapsody on a Theme of Paganini — 22'

Stravinsky
Symphony in Three Movements — 22'

Susan Bickley mezzo-soprano

Stephen Hough piano

BBC Symphony Orchestra
Leonard Slatkin conductor

Leonard Slatkin celebrates the music of his native America with three works by fellow countrymen and two written by Russian composers who ended their creative lives in America. Bernstein's serious side is represented by his First Symphony, based on Jeremiah's lamentations – a work which is new to the Proms.

This concert will be broadcast on BBC Television

PROM 43

Wednesday 22 August
7.30pm – c9.30pm
Price Code **B**

Rakhmaninov
Piano Concerto No. 3 in D minor *42'*

interval

Tchaikovsky
Symphony No. 1 in G minor,
'Winter Daydreams' *44'*

Lang Lang *piano*

St Petersburg Philharmonic
Yuri Temirkanov *conductor*

The St Petersburg Philharmonic Orchestra and its Music Director make a welcome return in a rarely heard symphony that captures the spirit of the Russian countryside, and the brilliant young Chinese pianist Lang Lang makes his London concerto debut in Rakhmaninov's fiendishly challenging Third Piano Concerto.

PROM 44 

Thursday 23 August
7.00pm – c9.15pm
Price Code **B**

NOTE TIME

Britten
Sinfonia da Requiem *20'*

Verdi
Four Sacred Pieces *38'*

interval

Beethoven
Piano Concerto No. 5
in E flat major, 'Emperor' *40'*

Yefim Bronfman *piano*

London Symphony Chorus
London Symphony Orchestra
Antonio Pappano *conductor*

Antonio Pappano, soon to take up the post of Music Director at the Royal Opera House, Covent Garden, has also recently forged an exciting relationship with the LSO. Together, they bring music by Britten composed in America – though commissioned to mark the 2,600th anniversary of Japan's imperial dynasty – and Verdi's late collection of sacred pieces, continuing this season's centenary survey (*see pages 42–45*). The Russian-born pianist Yefim Bronfman, now resident in America, joins them in Beethoven's dynamic final piano concerto.

5.30pm Pre-Prom Talk
John Evans on Britten in America

PROM 45 

Thursday 23 August
10.00pm – c11.25pm
Price Code **D**

LATE NIGHT

Ellington
Harlem *17'*

Gershwin
Lullaby for strings *8'*

Bernstein
Prelude, Fugue and Riffs *8'*

Michel Camilo
Piano Concerto *26'*
UK premiere

Martin Robertson *clarinet*

Michel Camilo *piano*

BBC Big Band
BBC Symphony Orchestra
Leonard Slatkin *conductor*

Under its new Chief Conductor, the BBC Symphony Orchestra will extend its repertoire, and here lets its hair down in a collaboration with the BBC Big Band for an evening of jazz-inspired music. The phenomenal Michel Camilo is the soloist in his own virtuosically demanding Piano Concerto (*see page 75*).

There will be no interval

PROM 46

Friday 24 August
7.30pm – c9.30pm
Price Code **B**

Schubert
Symphony No. 8 in B minor,
'Unfinished' *25'*

interval

Bruckner
Symphony No. 9 in D minor *61'*

NDR Symphony Orchestra,
Hamburg
Günter Wand *conductor*

Günter Wand, who has given such memorable performances of Bruckner's symphonies at the Proms in recent years, returns with the Hamburg-based orchestra of which he is Honorary Chief Conductor for Life to perform two great unfinished symphonies (*see page 86*).

PROM 47

Saturday 25 August
7.30pm – c9.30pm
Price Code **C**

Debussy
Prélude à L'après-midi d'un faune   10'

Martinů
Symphony No. 6, 'Fantaisies
symphoniques'   28'

interval

Brahms
Symphony No. 2 in D major   41'

Boston Symphony Orchestra
Bernard Haitink conductor

The Boston Symphony Orchestra
returns to the Proms after an absence
of 10 years in a pair of concerts
conducted by its Principal Guest
Conductor, Bernard Haitink, and
celebrating its former Music Director,
Serge Koussevitzky, on the 50th
anniversary of his death (see page 86).
The Koussevitzky-commissioned Sixth
Symphony of the Czech émigré
Bohuslav Martinů is flanked by Brahms's
'Pastoral' symphony and Debussy's
languorous orchestral impression of an
erotically charged Arcadian landscape.

🗨 **6.00pm Pre-Prom Talk**
Members of the Boston Symphony
Orchestra talk with Sue Knussen

PROM 48

Sunday 26 August
7.30pm – c9.20pm
Price Code **C**

Stravinsky
Symphony of Psalms   21'

interval

Ravel
Daphnis and Chloë   53'

Tanglewood Festival Chorus
Boston Symphony Orchestra
Bernard Haitink conductor

Stravinsky's *Symphony of Psalms* was
one of the many works commissioned
by Serge Koussevitzky during his 25
years as Music Director of the Boston
Symphony Orchestra (see *page 86*). It
prefaces Ravel's sensuously pastoral
ballet, composed for Diaghilev's Ballets
Russes. Bernard Haitink has made a
speciality of performing and recording
French repertory with this great
American orchestra. They are joined
here by the resident chorus from the
BSO's famous summer home at
Tanglewood in the Berkshire hills.

PROM 49

Monday 27 August
7.30pm – c9.35pm
Price Code **C**

Takemitsu
Ceremonial   8'

Prokofiev
Piano Concerto No. 3 in C major   29'

interval

Shostakovich
Symphony No. 5 in D minor   47'

Mayumi Miyata shō

Martha Argerich piano

NHK Symphony Orchestra
Charles Dutoit conductor

Japan's leading orchestra
visits the Proms with
Shostakovich's Fifth
Symphony, apocryphally
subtitled 'a Soviet artist's
creative reply to just
criticism'. They are joined for
Prokofiev's most popular piano
concerto by the legendary Martha
Argerich, who enjoyed such success in
the Schumann Concerto at last year's
Proms. Takemitsu's *Ceremonial* contains
a prominent part for the *shō*, a
traditional Japanese reed instrument.

This concert will be broadcast on BBC Television

♪ **1.00pm Proms Chamber Music**
See pages 110–11

PROM 50

Tuesday 28 August
7.30pm – c9.45pm
Price Code **C**

Wagner
The Mastersingers of Nuremberg –
Prelude to Act 3   7'

Schoenberg
Pelleas and Melisande   41'

interval

Skryabin
Prometheus: The Poem of Fire   24'

Wagner
Wotan's Farewell and Magic Fire Music
from 'Die Walküre'   17'

Alexander Toradze piano

Vladimir Vaneev baritone

Kirov Orchestra
Valery Gergiev conductor

Valery Gergiev and his Kirov Orchestra
return with favourite excerpts from
two of Wagner's music dramas,
Skryabin's feverish masterpiece –
arguably his greatest work – and the
lush and gorgeous sounds of an early
symphonic poem by Schoenberg, based
on the same Maeterlinck play that also
inspired Debussy's opera and suites of
incidental music by both Sibelius and
Fauré (see Prom 60).

Patrick Riou

Telephone booking opens on Friday 15 June: 020 7589 8212

PROM 51 →

Wednesday 29 August
7.00pm – c9.15pm
Price Code **A**

NOTE TIME

Schoenberg
Accompaniment to a Film Scene   8'

Pierre Boulez
Le visage nuptial*   30'

interval

Bartók
Duke Bluebeard's Castle   63'

Françoise Pollet soprano*
Katharina Kammerloher
mezzo-soprano*

Michelle DeYoung mezzo-soprano
László Polgár bass

BBC Singers (women's voices)
BBC Symphony Orchestra
Pierre Boulez conductor

Unlike many composers who escaped
to Hollywood when their European
existence became untenable,
Schoenberg never wrote a film score –
although he did compose this
accompaniment to an imaginary film
scene. Pierre Boulez directs his own
exquisite early work (setting texts by
René Char) for the first time at the
Proms, together with the only opera
by Bartók, a composer with whom he
shares a particular affinity (see page 63).

💬**5.30pm Pre-Prom Talk**
Pierre Boulez talks to Nicholas Kenyon

PROM 52 ←

Wednesday 29 August
10.00pm – c11.30pm
Price Code **D**

LATE NIGHT

Lambert
Prize Fight   9'

Finzi
Farewell to Arms   8'
Romance   6'

Britten
Nocturne   26'

Lambert, orch. Easterbrook
and Shipley
Piano Concerto (1924)   19'

Ian Bostridge tenor

Philip Fowke piano

Britten Sinfonia
Nicholas Cleobury conductor

Tenor Ian Bostridge
returns with the Britten
Sinfonia in a concert
marking this year's
Lambert and Finzi
anniversaries, featuring
Lambert's rarely heard early concerto
(completed from a piano sketch) and
Finzi's *Farewell to Arms*, a poetic variant
on the swords-into-ploughshares motif
whose two sections were composed
some 20 years apart. Britten's *Nocturne*,
commissioned by the BBC, is another
exploration of the English tradition.

There will be no interval

PROM 53

Thursday 30 August
7.30pm – c9.50pm
Price Code **B**

Mendelssohn
A Midsummer Night's Dream –
incidental music   40'

Haydn
Cello Concerto in C major   17'

interval

Dvořák
Symphony No. 9 in E minor,
'From the New World'   42'

Truls Mørk cello

Leipzig Gewandhaus Orchestra
Herbert Blomstedt conductor

One of the world's oldest performing
groups returns to the Proms with
Music Director Herbert Blomstedt
making his belated Proms debut. They
are joined by the Norwegian cellist
Truls Mørk for Haydn's ever-popular
concerto. Dvořák's final symphony is an
expression of his emotions on being far
from his homeland.

This concert will be broadcast on BBC Television

💬**6.00pm Pre-Prom Talk**
Herbert Blomstedt and the General
Manager of the Leipzig Gewandhaus
Orchestra, Andreas Schültz, in
conversation with Christopher Cook

PROM 54 → Ⓔ

Friday 31 August
7.00pm – c9.05pm
Price Code **B**

NOTE TIME

Sibelius
Violin Concerto in D minor   32'

interval

Mahler
Symphony No. 4 in G major   57'

Leonidas Kavakos violin

Ruth Ziesak soprano

Leipzig Gewandhaus Orchestra
Herbert Blomstedt conductor

The second of the Leipzig
Gewandhaus Orchestra's
two Proms features the
brilliant Greek violinist
Leonidas Kavakos in
Sibelius's lyrical Violin
Concerto (a work which he was
uniquely permitted to perform and
record in both its revised and its long-
suppressed original versions), and the
German soprano Ruth Ziesak in the
child's-eye vision of heaven that closes
Mahler's radiant Fourth Symphony.

💬**5.30pm Poetry Prom**
See page 131

PROM 55

Friday 31 August
10.00pm – c11.30pm
Price Code **D**

LATE NIGHT

Handel
Concerto grosso in D major,
Op. 6 No. 5 — *12'*

Vivaldi
Nisi Dominus, RV 608 — *23'*
Recorder Concerto in C major,
RV 444 — *10'*
Cessate, omai cessate, RV 684 — *13'*

Handel
Water Music – Suite in D — *12'*
'Va tacito' from 'Giulio Cesare' — *7'*

Andreas Scholl *counter-tenor*
Genevieve Lacey *recorder*

Australian Brandenburg Ensemble
Paul Dyer *director*

Andreas Scholl, the leading young counter-tenor who has made such an impact in Baroque opera at Glyndebourne, returns to the Proms in a pair of Vivaldi motets and a Handel aria, accompanied by a bright young Antipodean ensemble who punctuate the concert with instrumental pieces by the same composers.

There will be no interval

PROM 56

Saturday 1 September
7.30pm – c9.45pm
Price Code **A**

Enescu
Suite No. 1 — *29'*

Dvořák
Violin Concerto — *31'*

interval

Schumann
Symphony No. 1 in B flat major,
'Spring' — *33'*

Sarah Chang *violin*

London Philharmonic Orchestra
Kurt Masur *conductor*

The London Philharmonic Orchestra and its Principal Conductor perform a neo-classical suite by a composer who divided his time between France and his native Romania, Dvořák's Violin Concerto and Schumann's 'Spring' Symphony, a work which was inspired by Beethoven's 'Pastoral' and seeks to transplant its classicism into a more overtly romantic sound world.

PROM 57

Sunday 2 September
7.00pm – c9.10pm
Price Code **A**

NOTE TIME

Strauss
Till Eulenspiegel — *15'*

Bartók
Piano Concerto No. 3 — *25'*

interval

Julian Philips
Out of Light — *18'*
BBC commission: world premiere

Rakhmaninov
Symphonic Dances — *35'*

Andreas Haefliger *piano*

BBC National Orchestra of Wales
Tadaaki Otaka *conductor*

Bartók's Third Piano Concerto and Rakhmaninov's *Symphonic Dances* are both works composed after their respective composers' migrations to America. Julian Philips is a young composer who made a splash when the BBC National Orchestra of Wales performed his *Strange Seas* – which led to this, his first Proms commission (see *page 73*). The BBC NOW and its Japanese Conductor Laureate raise the curtain on the concert with Strauss's roguish trickster.

6.00pm Pre-Prom Talk
Julian Philips talks to Edward Seckerson

PROM 58

Monday 3 September
7.00pm – c9.05pm
Price Code **B**

NOTE TIME

Prokofiev
Cinderella – suite — *c30'*

Glière
Concerto for Coloratura Soprano
(arr. for trumpet) — *13'*

interval

Dvořák
Symphony No. 7 in D minor — *38'*

Sergei Nakariakov *trumpet*

Czech Philharmonic Orchestra
Vladimir Ashkenazy *conductor*

The Czech Philharmonic Orchestra returns to the Proms with its current Music Director in Dvořák's great symphony, imbued with the folk spirit of his Czech homeland, plus music from Prokofiev's *Cinderella* ballet and a new arrangement of Glière's mellifluous vocal concerto, transcribed for virtuoso trumpet.

1.00pm Proms Chamber Music
See pages 110–11

PROM 59 ⓖ

Monday 3 September
10.00pm – c11.20pm
Price Code **D**

LATE NIGHT

Schoenberg
Verklärte Nacht · 30'
Pierrot lunaire · 36'

Claron McFadden *sprechstimme*

Nash Ensemble
Pierre-André Valade *conductor*

Claron McFadden

Two nocturnal works by Schoenberg are aptly coupled in a late-night concert continuing our season's survey of the composer's music on the 50th anniversary of his death (see pages 50–52). *Verklärte Nacht* ('Transfigured Night'), Schoenberg's sumptuous instrumental response to a Richard Dehmel poem about a man forgiving his lover's infidelity, is contrasted with the menacing and darkly expressionistic world of *Pierrot lunaire*, a set of 'three times seven' half-sung songs about a moonstruck, lovesick clown.

There will be no interval

PROM 60 ⓔ

Tuesday 4 September
7.30pm – c9.45pm
Price Code **B**

Fauré
Pelleas and Melisande · 17'

Henri Dutilleux
Tout un monde lointain … · 29'

interval

Roussel
Bacchus and Ariadne – Suite No. 2 · 19'

Debussy
La mer · 24'

Steven Isserlis *cello*

Czech Philharmonic Orchestra
Vladimir Ashkenazy *conductor*

We celebrate the 85th birthday of Henri Dutilleux this year with a performance of his 1970 cello concerto, set in a context of French music of earlier years. Fauré's incidental music to *Pelleas and Melisande* was composed for a London production of Maeterlinck's play in 1898, four years before Debussy turned it into an opera; Debussy's own set of symphonic seascapes was completed while he was on holiday in Eastbourne in 1905; while Roussel's dazzling suite is drawn from his 1931 ballet on a familiar mythological tale set on the island of Naxos.

PROM 61

Wednesday 5 September
7.30pm – c9.40pm
Price Code **B**

Mozart
Symphony No. 32 in G major, K318 · 9'
Piano Concerto No. 25 in C major, K503 · 30'

interval

Stravinsky
Concerto in D for strings · 12'

Schubert
Symphony No. 4 in C minor, 'Tragic' · 31'

Alfred Brendel *piano*

Scottish Chamber Orchestra
Sir Charles Mackerras *conductor*

Alred Brendel

The Scottish Chamber Orchestra and its Conductor Laureate have collaborated successfully with Alfred Brendel on a series of performances and recordings of the Mozart piano concertos, and bring the grandest of them all to the Proms, along with an Italianate symphony from the late 1770s. The classical strand continues with Schubert's rarely-heard early symphony and Stravinsky's neo-classical string concerto.

PROM 62

Thursday 6 September
7.30pm – c9.35pm
Price Code **A**

Ravel
Alborada del gracioso · 8'

Satie, arr. Debussy
Deux gymnopédies · 7'

Debussy, arr. Adams
Le livre de Baudelaire · 22'

interval

John Adams
Naive and Sentimental Music · 50'
London premiere

Dame Felicity Lott *soprano*

BBC Symphony Orchestra
John Adams *conductor*

Felicity Lott

John Adams, in his first concert with the BBC Symphony Orchestra, presents his most recent orchestral work (see pages 34–36), alongside his own arrangements of Debussy songs, and Debussy's orchestration of a pair of Satie's gymnastic *Gymnopédies*. Ravel's Spanish jester gets the concert off to a sunny start.

♪ **6.00pm Composer Portrait**
John Adams. *See page 133*

PROM 63

Friday 7 September
7.00pm – c9.05pm
Price Code **C**

Wagner
Overture 'Tannhäuser' *13'*

Elliott Carter
Partita *18'*

interval

Mahler
Symphony No. 1 in D major *55'*

Chicago Symphony Orchestra
Daniel Barenboim conductor

The Chicago Symphony Orchestra returns for a pair of concerts featuring three of Daniel Barenboim's specialities: Mahler symphonies, Wagner operas, and new music, which he has done so much to support and commission. He enjoys an especially close relationship with the veteran American composer Elliott Carter, whose first opera *What Next?* he premiered in Berlin in 1999, having premiered Carter's *Partita* – the work he here brings to the Proms – with the Chicago Symphony Orchestra five years before.

PROM 64

Friday 7 September
10.00pm – c11.30pm
Price Code **D**

Sir Harrison Birtwistle
Sonance 2000 *8'*

Britten
Hymn to St Cecilia *12'*

Takemitsu
Garden Rain *8'*

Sir Harrison Birtwistle
New work for brass *c5'*
BBC commission: world premiere

Three Latin Motets from
'The Last Supper' *13'*
UK premiere live performance

Takemitsu
Signals from Heaven *6'*

Stravinsky
Mass *17'*

London Brass and Reeds
BBC Singers
Stephen Cleobury conductor

A concert of vocal and brass music featuring new and recent works by Birtwistle (see *page 71*), including the first live UK performance of the Three Latin Motets that are heard on tape in his latest opera, *The Last Supper*. Stravinsky's great neo-classical setting of the mass and Britten's Cecilian ode were both composed in America.

There will be no interval

PROM 65

Saturday 8 September
7.30pm – c9.40pm
Price Code **C**

Augusta Read Thomas
Aurora, for piano and orchestra *c15'*
UK premiere

interval

Mahler
Symphony No. 7 *79'*

Chicago Symphony Orchestra
Daniel Barenboim piano/conductor

Daniel Barenboim doubles as both conductor and pianist in a new concertante work written especially for him (see *page 77*). As Composer-in-Residence in Chicago, Augusta Read Thomas has had works premiered by both Boulez and Barenboim. Mahler's darkest symphony promises to explore the virtuosity of one of the world's greatest orchestras.

💬 **6.00pm Pre-Prom Talk**
Augusta Read Thomas

PROM 66

Sunday 9 September
7.30pm – c9.50pm
Price Code **B**

Beethoven
Triple Concerto *35'*

interval

Beethoven
Symphony No. 9 in D minor,
'Choral' *70'*

Elisabeth Batiashvili violin
Alban Gerhardt cello
Steven Osborne piano

Amanda Roocroft soprano
Catherine Wyn-Rogers mezzo-soprano
Kurt Streit tenor
Peter Rose bass

London Philharmonic Choir
BBC Scottish Symphony Orchestra
Osmo Vänskä conductor

Osmo Vänskä

Three young artists from BBC Radio 3's 'New Generations' scheme return to the Proms for Beethoven's Triple Concerto, and the relationship between the BBC Scottish Symphony Orchestra and Osmo Vänskä reaches its climax in the 'Choral' Symphony – Beethoven's great ode to brotherhood and joy – without which no Proms season would be complete.

💬 **5.45pm Audience Forum**
See page 134

Eric Thorburn

PROM 67 

Monday 10 September
7.30pm – c9.50pm
Price Code **A**

Schoenberg
A Survivor from Warsaw — 8'

Alexander Goehr
… second musical offering (GFH 2001)
BBC commission: world premiere — c28'

interval

Vaughan Williams
A Sea Symphony — 66'

Narrator to be announced

Joan Rodgers *soprano*
Simon Keenlyside *baritone*

**Trinity College of
Music Chamber Choir
BBC Symphony Chorus
Philharmonia Chorus
BBC Symphony Orchestra
Leonard Slatkin** *conductor*

Vaughan Williams's monumental Walt Whitman setting and Schoenberg's harrowing but eloquent and uplifting account of Jewish courage in the face of death frame Alexander Goehr's latest commission, a double concerto for orchestra in homage to Handel (see *page 72*).

♪**1.00pm Proms Chamber Music**
See pages 110–11

💬**6.00pm Pre-Prom Talk**
Alexander Goehr and Christopher Cook

PROM 68 

Tuesday 11 September
7.00pm – c9.15pm
Price Code **C**

NOTE TIME

Beethoven
Overture 'The Creatures
of Prometheus' — 5'
Piano Concerto No. 4 in G major — 34'

interval

Berlioz
Symphonie fantastique — 53'

Hélène Grimaud *piano*

**Orchestre de Paris
Christoph Eschenbach** *conductor*

Hélène Grimaud

Christoph Eschenbach, who was recently appointed Music Director in Philadelphia, has been building a new profile for France's leading orchestra. Both he and Hélène Grimaud are appearing at the Proms for the first time this season. Beethoven's Orpheus-inspired concerto and ballet overture preface Berlioz's colourful symphony, one of the masterpieces of French music, which ranges from the gently pastoral to the grotesque.

PROM 69 

Tuesday 11 September
10.00pm – c11.30pm
Price Code **D**

LATE NIGHT

PERCUSSION OLD & NEW

Programme to include

György Ligeti
Síppal, Dobbal, Nádihegedüvel — 12'

**Music by Xenakis and
traditional African drumming**

Katalin Károlyi *mezzo-soprano*
4-mality
Other artists to be announced

György Ligeti's settings of Sándor Weöres's nonsense poems, *Síppal, Dobbal, Nádihegedüvel*, caused a sensation at the work's London premiere on the South Bank in February. Here the singer for whom the songs were composed appears with the virtuoso young percussion group 4-mality, led by BBC Young Musician 1998, Adrian Spillett. Alongside two pieces by 4-mality members Stephen Whibley (*Monsoon*) and Jan Bradley (*In-Line*), the programme will include both a tribute to the exiled Greek composer Iannis Xenakis, who died in February, and samples of the African drumming that has exerted such an influence on Ligeti.

There will be no interval

PROM 70

Wednesday 12 September
7.30pm – c9.20pm
Price Code **C**

Berlioz
Overture 'Benvenuto Cellini' — 11'

Schumann
Symphony No. 2 in C major — 37'

interval

Stravinsky
The Rite of Spring — 34'

**Orchestre de Paris
Christoph Eschenbach** *conductor*

This year's Proms have explored the seasons, the countryside and nature. Stravinsky's pagan ritual, which famously scandalised its first Parisian audience, is an unsurpassed evocation of the savage power of spring's awakening, with its musical roots planted deep in Russian folk tradition.

PROM 71

Thursday 13 September
7.30pm – c9.25pm
Price Code **B**

Sibelius
The Oceanides   10'

Tippett
The Rose Lake   28'

interval

Beethoven
Symphony No. 6 in F major,
'Pastoral'   42'

London Symphony Orchestra
Sir Colin Davis conductor

Beethoven's Sixth Symphony is surely the apogee of the pastoral. Here it is prefaced by Sibelius's late tone-poem, which he premiered in America, and the late Michael Tippett's shimmering evocation of a Senegalese lakeside view, which was composed for tonight's orchestra and conductor.

This concert will be broadcast on BBC Television

PROM 72 Ⓖ Ⓔ

Friday 14 September
7.30pm – c9.00pm
Price Code **B**

Verdi
Requiem   84'

Fiorenza Cedolins soprano
Luciana D'Intino mezzo-soprano
Vincenzo La Scola tenor
Carlo Colombara bass

Bologna Opera Chorus
London Voices
Royal Philharmonic Orchestra
Daniele Gatti conductor

An all-Italian cast and a Bolognese opera chorus join the Royal Philharmonic Orchestra and its Music Director Daniele Gatti in what promises to be a dramatic and powerful performance of Verdi's humanist Requiem, bringing to a climax our commemoration of the composer's centenary.

There will be no interval

PROM 73

Saturday 15 September
7.30pm – c10.30pm
Price Code **E**

THE LAST NIGHT OF THE PROMS 2001

Verdi
Overture 'La forza del destino'   8'
Chorus of the Hebrew Slaves
from 'Nabucco'   5'

Finzi
The Fall of the Leaf   10'

Ravel
Shéhérazade   17'

Lambert
The Rio Grande*   14'

interval

John Adams
Short Ride in a Fast Machine   5'

Ives, orch. Schuman
Variations on 'America'   7'

Canteloube
Songs of the Auvergne – selection   10'

Sousa
Liberty Bell – march   3'

Elgar
Pomp and Circumstance March
No. 1 in D major   5'

Henry Wood
Fantasia on British Sea-Songs   12'
concluding with

Arne, arr. Sargent
Rule, Britannia!   5'

Parry, orch. Elgar
Jerusalem   2'

Frederica von Stade mezzo-soprano

Alice Coote mezzo-soprano*

Paul Lewis piano

BBC Singers
BBC Symphony Chorus
BBC Symphony Orchestra
Leonard Slatkin conductor

Frederica
von Stade

The strands of the season are drawn together on the Last Night. The Hebrew Slaves mourn their exile in Verdi's most famous chorus; Finzi is represented by his last orchestral work, and Lambert by his most famous. John Adams's virtuoso showpiece ushers in an American flavour to the second half, with Ives's cheeky variations on a well-known tune and Sousa's march, made famous by a certain British comedy show. A great American mezzo-soprano makes her Proms debut in a selection of Canteloube's delightful song arrangements. And Leonard Slatkin holds the proceedings together, bringing his own unique twist to British music's greatest institution.

This concert will be broadcast on BBC Television

Marcia Lieberman

BBC Proms in the Park

The BBC presents the sixth season of Proms in the Park, bringing the traditional atmosphere of the Last Night of the Proms to audiences in London, Liverpool, Gateshead and St Austell. All four concerts culminate in live big-screen link-ups with the Royal Albert Hall.

BBC Proms in the Park, London

José Carreras, international opera star and one third of 'The Three Tenors', and jazz master Jools Holland lead the celebrity line-up joining the BBC Concert Orchestra and the Royal Choral Society under conductor Robin Stapleton for the main part of the evening's entertainment, hosted yet again by the inimitable Terry Wogan.

*Saturday 15 September
Hyde Park. Gates open
4.00pm; entertainment
on stage from 5.30pm*

THE ROYAL PARKS

Tickets: £15.00, available now (plus booking fee) from Ticketmaster on 0870 514 3109 (lines open 24 hours a day; calls charged at national rate) or from the Royal Albert Hall Box Office by post or fax, using the Booking Form (*facing page 122*), or by phone on 020 7589 8212 (lines open from 15 June, 9.00am–9.00pm daily)

Corporate hospitality facilities are available. Call Charles Webb on 01484 435569.

RENAULT – Official sponsor of Proms in the Park, London, and CBBC Prom in the Park

CBBC Prom in the Park

A family fun afternoon hosted by *Blue Peter's* Matt Baker and Simon Thomas, with Faye Tozer from Steps, and featuring Brits Award-winning chart band a1 plus The Tweenies and other stars and friends from CBBC. Rumon Gamba conducts the BBC Philharmonic.

Sunday 16 September

Hyde Park, London. Gates open 2.00pm; entertainment on stage from 3.00pm

Tickets: £10.00 (adults), £6 (children 3–16); under-3s free. Book by phone (plus booking fee) on 0870 533 433 (national rate)

BBC Proms in the Park, Liverpool

Liverpool joins the Last Night festivities for a second year. The Royal Liverpool Philharmonic Orchestra will be conducted by Gerard Schwarz, and the concert will end with a grand fireworks finale.

*Saturday 15 September
William Brown Street, off St George's Hall Plateau. Gates open 5.00pm; entertainment on stage from 6.00pm*

Tickets: £10.00, available from the Philharmonic Hall Box Office on 0151 709 3789

BBC Proms in the Park, Gateshead

One of the inaugural events for Music Centre Gateshead (opening in 2003 as the centrepiece of the £250m Gateshead Quays development), this Tyneside musical feast unites Northumbrian Pipes virtuoso Kathryn Tickell with the Northern Sinfonia and a host of other well-known Northern musicians.

*Saturday 15 September
Baltic Square. Gates open 6.15pm; entertainment on stage from 7.15pm*

Tickets: £12.00, available from Freephone 0800 953 0070

BBC Proms in the Park, Cornwall

The BBC National Orchestra of Wales and conductor Wayne Marshall are joined by the stunning young British cellist, and former BBC Young Musician, Natalie Clein for a celebratory concert in the open-air amphitheatre in front of the awesome giant 'biomes' of the newly opened Eden Project, the biggest set of greenhouses in the world.

*Saturday 15 September
Eden Project, St Austell, Cornwall*

Tickets: call Freephone 0800 052 1812 for details of times and ticket prices

Please note: all BBC Proms in the Park events are outdoors and tickets are unreserved. In the interest of safety, please do not bring glass items or picnic furniture.

BBC Proms in the Park, London, will be broadcast live on BBC Radio 2. The Liverpool, Gateshead and St Austell concerts will be broadcast on their nearest BBC Local Radio stations (Merseyside, Newcastle and Cornwall). Highlights of all four Proms in the Park will be shown as part of BBC1 and BBC2's live coverage of the Last Night of the Proms

PICTURED
Natalie Clein (*below*) joins conductor Wayne Marshall (*bottom far left*) in the garden at Eden; Kathryn Tickell (*bottom*) plays her pipes on Tyneside

Proms Chamber Music

Mondays at 1.00pm
Lecture Theatre, Victoria and Albert Museum
Broadcast live on BBC Radio 3
and repeated the following Sunday at 1.00pm

The BBC Proms and the Victoria and Albert Museum continue their popular collaboration, presenting eight Monday lunchtime concerts highlighting Proms artists, themes and anniversaries in the intimate setting of the Lecture Theatre at the V&A, a short walk from the Royal Albert Hall.

Performing Art

Once again, arts broadcaster Christopher Cook unveils some of the riches of the V&A's collection, with guest experts from the museum (*see page 132*). Each event will focus on a particular object that relates to the music being performed.

Performing Art talks begin at 12.15pm, last about 20 minutes and are free to Proms Chamber Music ticket-holders.

Performing Art talks will be recorded for broadcast on Radio 3 as interval features during each Thursday's Prom.

How to Book

All tickets are £6.00 and include Museum admission. To avoid disappointment, please book in advance.

Before the day of the concert all bookings should be made with the Royal Albert Hall Box Office, *either* using the Booking Form (facing page 122) *or* by telephone or in person (from Friday 15 June).

On the day of the concert tickets can only be bought (subject to availability) at the V&A, Exhibition Road entrance (*see map on page 115*).

The museum and its restaurant open at 10.00am.

For details of the Poetry Proms, Proms Composer Portraits, Pre-Prom Talks and the BBC Proms Lecture, see pages 131–4.

PCM 1
Monday 23 July
1.00pm – c2.00pm

Couperin
Concerts royaux – quatrième concert *12'*

Rameau
Rossignols amoureux *5'*

Couperin
Le Rossignol en amour *4'*

Montéclair
Pan and Syrinx *18'*

Rameau
Pièces de clavecin en concerts – premier concert *10'*

Sophie Daneman *soprano*
Nancy Hadden *flute*
Alison Bury *violin*
Erin Headley *viola da gamba*
Lucy Carolan *harpsichord*

As the Proms embark on a season featuring the pastoral, the chamber music series opens in the enchanted world of the French Baroque. Here in 'flourishing Arcady', like the sumptuous setting of a Watteau painting, the nightingales sing and the amorous god Pan pursues the hapless nymph Syrinx.

PCM 2
Monday 30 July
1.00pm – c2.00pm

Finzi
Let Us Garlands Bring *15'*

Wolf
Mörike Lieder – selections *7'*

Britten
The Salley Gardens *3'*
The Plough Boy *2'*
The Miller of Dee *2'*

Vaughan Williams
Silent Noon *4'*

Butterworth
Six Songs from 'A Shropshire Lad' *15'*

Sir Thomas Allen *baritone*
Malcolm Martineau *piano*

High hills, leafy woods and winding country lanes shape the landscape of the English pastoral imagination. In a recital which celebrates the nostalgic moment, Butterworth evokes a world of endless summer afternoons, Britten reinvents English folk song and centenary composer Gerald Finzi pays tribute to Shakespeare.

PCM 3
Monday 6 August
1.00pm – c2.00pm

Dvořák
String Quartet in F major, Op. 96, 'American' *25'*

Bartók
String Quartet No. 6 *30'*

Henschel Quartet

Exile has many faces. For Dvořák, his time in America was a musical adventure, a stimulating glimpse of the new world. Bartók was about to flee to America from war-threatened Europe when he wrote his last quartet, full of apprehension and resignation – an autumnal farewell.

PCM 4
Monday 13 August
1.00pm – c2.00pm

Busoni, arr. Stein
Berceuse élégiaque   8'

Berg
Four Pieces, Op. 5   8'

Schoenberg, arr. Webern
Chamber Symphony No. 1   21'

J. Strauss II, arr.
Schoenberg
Roses from the South
– waltz   10'

Michael Collins clarinet
John Constable piano
London Sinfonietta
Diego Masson conductor

In the 50th anniversary year
of the death of Schoenberg,
a re-creation of repertoire
performed at his Viennese
Society for Private Musical
Performances. Dedicated to
contemporary music, but
always short of funds, the
Society flourished with a
small chamber ensemble –
including a harmonium –
and a lot of imagination!

PCM 5
Monday 20 August
1.00pm – c2.00pm

Chopin
Barcarolle in F sharp minor,
Op. 60   9'
Études Op. 25 Nos. 7, 8
& 12   10

Debussy
Images, Book 2   14'

György Ligeti
Études – selections, including
Galamb borong, Automne
à Varsovie and No. 18   12
UK premiere of Étude No. 18

Pierre-Laurent Aimard
piano

'What wonders Cézanne
accomplished with his
harmonies of colour,' says
Ligeti, and he also
acknowledges a debt to
Chopin and Debussy –
'composers who thought
pianistically' – in writing his
brilliant, virtuoso Études.
Ligeti's latest Étude crowns
a recital rich in pictorial
associations (pastoral and
exile included).

PCM 6
Monday 27 August
1.00pm – c2.00pm

Stravinsky
The Soldier's Tale   55'

Samuel West narrator
Britten Sinfonia Soloists
Nicholas Cleobury conductor

A concert performance of
Stravinsky's astringent parable
from the Jazz Age, composed
when he was cut off from his
homeland by war and
revolution. It charts the
fortunes of an ill-fated soldier
who gambles wildly with the
Devil for riches, happiness and,
ultimately, his very soul.

PCM 7
Monday 3 September
1.00pm – c2.00pm

O Fragrant Rose

**English vocal music of the
14th, 15th and 21st
centuries, including**

John Casken
To the Lovers' Well   10'
BBC commission: world premiere

Orlando Consort

In the first great age of English
music, medieval composers
were irresistibly drawn to
setting texts in honour of
the Virgin Mary. Many chose
poems rich in pastoral allusion,
and some of the most
exquisite anonymous works
are here paired with pieces
by Dunstaple, Plummer
and an intriguing, specially
commissioned new work
by John Casken.

PCM 8
Monday 10 September
1.00pm – c2.00pm

Schubert
The Shepherd on the Rock 12'

Piano Trio in B flat major,
D898   40'

Emma Bell soprano
Ronald van Spaendonck
clarinet
Elisabeth Batiashvili violin
Alban Gerhardt cello
Steven Osborne piano

Radio 3 New Generation
artists close the series with
Schubert's delightful vision of
the pastoral, tinged with loss,
and one of his greatest, most
radiant chamber works.
Schumann declared that 'one
glance at the Trio by Schubert
and the world shines fresh and
new again'.

Special Offers

To claim any of these discounts, complete the priority Booking Form (facing page 122), ticking the appropriate discount box, or mention the relevant offer when booking tickets by phone or in person where applicable (from Friday 15 June). All offers are subject to availability.

Proms Explorer

Each season the Proms offer an incredible variety of concerts for you to enjoy, with music both old and new, artists from home and abroad, and a huge range of pieces from operas and symphonies to *a cappella* **choruses and chamber works. The choice can seem overwhelming.**

But that's exactly what makes the Proms such fun to explore. The articles in this Guide are there to help you plan your Prom-going, navigating you through the year's themes, works by composers you may not know and artists you may never have heard before. Alternatively, let us do the choosing for you, with the following list of concerts guaranteed to lead you down new paths as well as through familiar terrain.

Choose three or four concerts and save 10% – plus we'll give you each a free programme. Choose five concerts, and save 15% – plus we'll give you free tickets to any one of the selected Late Night Proms listed below.

All you have to do is select your concerts from the list below, then complete the special section on Part 2 of the Booking Form (facing page 122) or mention your chosen offer when booking by phone (from 15 June). Note that Explorer offers apply to Stalls, Front Circle and Rear Circle tickets only, and that you must book the same number of tickets in the same seating area for each concert.

Explorer offers are only open until Friday 6 July. So book early.

PROM 4
Monday 23 July, 7.30pm
Weber, Vaughan Williams, Schubert

PROM 9
Friday 27 July, 7.30pm
Rubbra, Ravel, Elgar

PROM 18
Friday 3 August, 7.00pm
Varèse, Bernstein, Ravel

PROM 27
Thursday 9 August, 7.30pm
Grieg: Peer Gynt

PROM 32
Tuesday 14 August, 7.00pm
The Great Escape:
Hollywood's Golden Age

PROM 36
Friday 17 August, 7.30pm
Ligeti, Stravinsky, Bartók

PROM 42
Tuesday 21 August, 7.30pm
Copland, Barber, Bernstein, Rakhmaninov, Stravinsky

PROM 54
Friday 31 August, 7.00pm
Sibelius, Mahler

PROM 60
Tuesday 4 September, 7.30pm
Fauré, Dutilleux, Roussel, Debussy

PROM 72
Friday 14 September, 7.30pm
Verdi: Requiem

Late Night Proms
Five-concert Explorers are entitled to free tickets to any one of the following Late Night Proms:

PROM 19
Friday 3 August, 10.00pm
The Later Prom

PROM 33
Tuesday 14 August, 10.00pm
An Evening of Klezmer & Gypsy Music

PROM 55
Friday 31 August, 10.00pm
Vivaldi, Handel

Same Day Savers

Go to an evening concert, stay on for the Late Night Prom, and save £2.00 on your Late Night ticket.

Note that Same Day Savers do not apply to Arena and Gallery standing areas or to Circle Restricted View seats.

Premieres

As part of the Proms commitment to new music, readers of this Guide are offered an exclusive discount of £3.00 off normal ticket prices for the following Proms, all of which include premieres (see 'New Music', pages 70–77). Bookings must be made using the Booking Form facing page 122.

Note that Premiere offers do not apply to Arena and Gallery standing areas or to Circle Restricted View seats.

PROM 8
Thursday 26 July, 7.30pm
James MacMillan:
Birds of Rhiannon
BBC commission: world premiere

PROM 12
Sunday 29 July, 7.30pm
Sally Beamish: Knotgrass Elegy
BBC commission: world premiere

PROM 14
Tuesday 31 July, 7.00pm
Stuart MacRae:
Violin Concerto
world premiere

PROM 20
Saturday 4 August, 7.30pm
John Tavener: Song of
the Cosmos *world premiere*

PROM 28
Friday 10 August, 7.30pm
Poul Ruders: Studium
BBC/Danish National Radio SO commission: UK premiere

PROM 30
Sunday 12 August, 7.30pm
Pierre Boulez: Notation VII
UK premiere
Tobias Picker: Cello Concerto
BBC commission: world premiere

PROM 67
Monday 10 September, 7.30pm
Alexander Goehr: ... second
musical offering (GFH 2001)
BBC commission: world premiere

Group Bookings

Groups of 10 or more can receive a discount of 10% on the price of Stalls, Front Circle or Rear Circle tickets to the following Proms:

PROM 4
Monday 23 July, 7.30pm
Weber, Vaughan Williams,
Schubert

PROM 13
Monday 30 July, 7.30pm
Nielsen, Prokofiev,
Vaughan Williams

PROM 21
Sunday 5 August, 2.30pm
The 'Nation's Favourite' Prom

PROM 25
Tuesday 7 August, 7.30pm
Dukas, Tchaikovsky, Lyadov,
Musorgsky, orch. Ravel

PROM 26
Wednesday 8 August, 7.00pm Haydn: The Seasons

PROM 32
Tuesday 14 August, 7.00pm
The Great Escape:
Hollywood's Golden Age

PROM 33
Tuesday 14 August, 10.00pm
An Evening of Klezmer
& Gypsy Music

PROM 37
Saturday 18 August, 7.00pm
Smetana, Dvořák, Rodrigo,
Johann Strauss II

PROM 42
Tuesday 21 August, 7.30pm
Copland, Barber, Bernstein,
Rakhmaninov, Stravinsky

PROM 58
Monday 3 September, 7.00pm
Prokofiev, Glière, Dvořák

PROM 72
Friday 14 September, 7.30pm Verdi: Requiem

For more information, call the Group Booking Information Line: 020 7838 3108

Under-16s

If you're under 16 years old, you can buy half-price tickets (in any seated area) to the following Proms:

PROM 10
Saturday 28 July, 11.00am
Blue Peter Prom

PROM 21
Sunday 5 August, 2.30pm
The 'Nation's Favourite' Prom

PROM 29
Saturday 11 August, 7.00pm
Messiaen: organ works,
Turangalîla Symphony

PROM 37
Saturday 18 August, 7.00pm
Smetana, Dvořák, Rodrigo,
Johann Strauss II

PROM 70
Wednesday 12 September, 7.30pm
Berlioz, Schumann, Stravinsky

Getting to the Royal Albert Hall

**The following buses stop
where indicated:**
No. 9 to Charing Cross
No. 10 to Euston and King's Cross
No. 52 to Victoria

**The following buses stop
where indicated:**
No. 9 to Hammersmith
No. 10 to Hammersmith
No. 52 to Notting Hill and Willesden

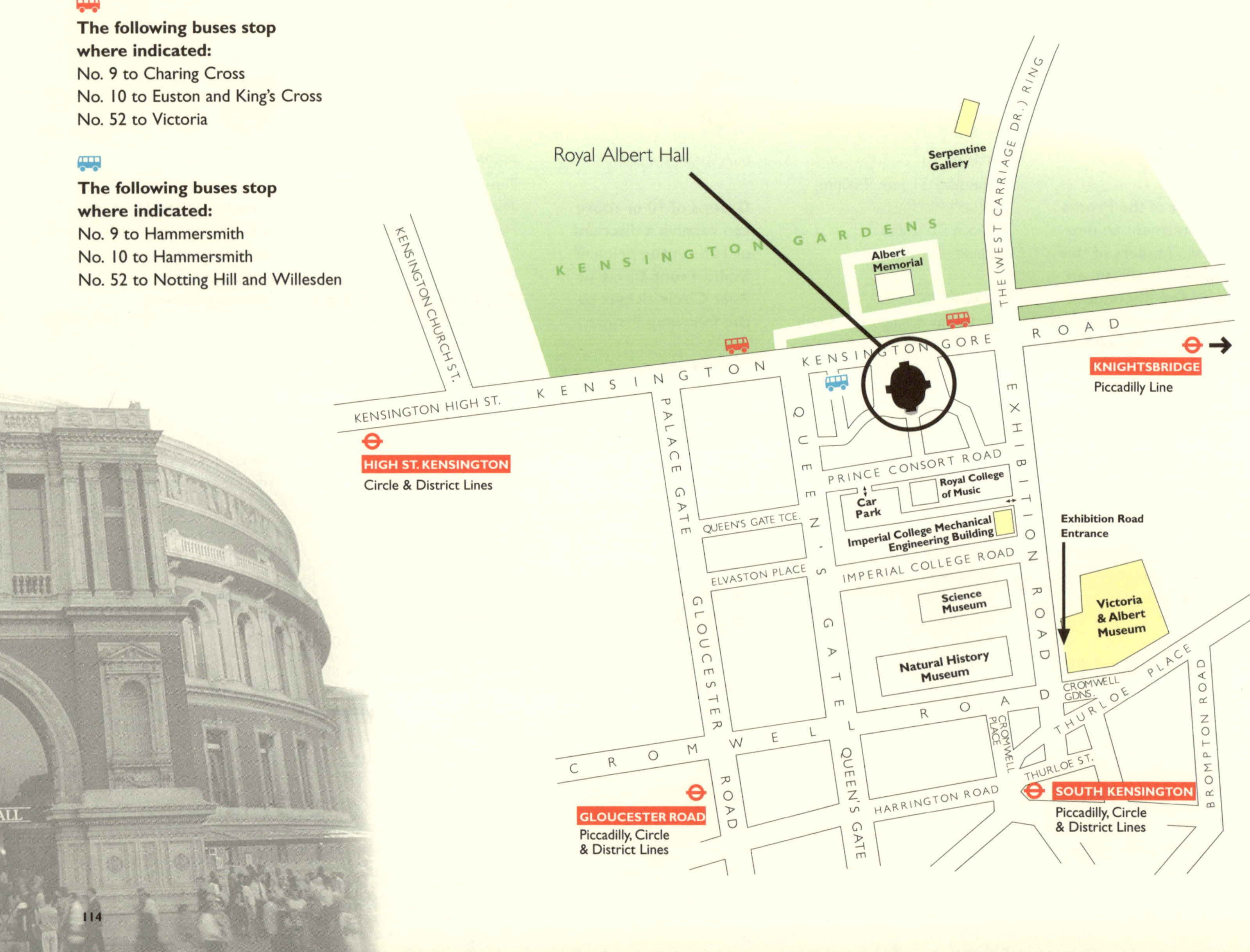

At the Proms

Doors open 45 minutes before each concert.

Latecomers will not be admitted into the auditorium until there is a suitable break in the music. There is a video monitor with digital audio relay in the foyer at Door 6.

Bags and coats may be left in the cloakrooms at Door 4 (ground level), Door 8 (circle level) and within the Arena corridor. Folding chairs and hand-luggage larger than a briefcase are not allowed in the auditorium.

Dos and Don'ts Eating, drinking and smoking are not permitted inside the auditorium, and the use of cameras, video cameras and recording equipment is strictly forbidden. Mobile phones and watch alarms must be turned off.

Children under 5 In consideration of our audience and artists, children under the age of 5 are not allowed in the auditorium. Children between the ages of 5 and 16 are positively encouraged (*see Special Offers, pages 112–13*).

Car Parking A limited number of parking spaces is available from 6.00pm in the Imperial College Car Park (Prince Consort or Exhibition Road entrances). These can be booked in advance (priced £6.00) by ticking the appropriate column on the Booking Form (facing page 122) or by telephoning the Box Office (open 9.00am–9.00pm daily, from 15 June) on 020 7589 8212. Please note that, if attending both early-evening and late-night concerts, only one parking fee is payable.

Dress Code There is no dress code at the Proms.

Eating and drinking at the Hall

Restaurants
The Royal Albert Hall has three restaurants catering for all tastes, from light meals to a three-course dining experience. All restaurants are open two hours prior to the start of the performance.

The Elgar Restaurant offers a two- or three-course fixed price menu with full table service. Tables in the Elgar Restaurant are bookable in advance on 020 7589 8900. Entrance is via Door 8 to Circle Level.

The Prince Consort Wine Bar offers light meals, including sandwiches, salad bowls and afternoon tea in an informal setting. Entrance is via Door 2 to Grand Tier Level.

The Victoria Room Brasserie offers a range of light meals, salads and desserts in the café style. Entrance is via Door 2 to Circle Level.

Box hospitality can be pre-ordered by telephoning 020 7589 5666. Please allow two working days' notice.

Bars
Bars are located on every floor and all offer a full range of alcoholic and soft drinks, hot beverages, ice cream and sandwiches.

The Champagne and North Circle Bars open two hours prior to the start of the performance. Both offer a range of sandwiches and a small amount of seating is available. Enter via Door 2 to Grand Tier level and Circle level respectively.

The following bars are also available and open one hour prior to the start of the performance:

Proms Bar (located in the sub-basement) – enter via Door 2

Door 6 Bars (located at ground level) – enter via Door 6

The Porch Bar – enter via Door 9 to Grand Tier level

The Second Tier Bar – enter via Door 4 to Second Tier level.

Please note that you are not permitted to consume your own food and drink in the Hall. In the interests of Health and Safety, glasses and bottles are not allowed in the auditorium except as part of Box hospitality ordered through the Hall's caterers.

Information for disabled concert-goers

Access at the Proms

Call the **Access Information Line** on **020 7589 3853** for advice on facilities for disabled concert-goers (including car-parking) at all Proms venues, or if you have any special requirements. Dedicated staff will be available 10.00am–5.00pm, Mon–Fri.

Wheelchair access is available at all Proms venues, but advance booking is advised.

The Royal Albert Hall has up to 14 spaces bookable in the Stalls for wheelchair-users and their companions (entrance via Door 8). End-of-aisle places and front-row platform spaces either side of the stage are priced as Stalls seats; rear platform places are priced as Front Circle seats. When filling in the Booking Form, tick your preferred price range (*ie* Stalls or Front Circle) and enter number of places required under the 'Wheelchair space' column.

For unticketed events (*ie* Poetry Proms, Composer Portraits and the Proms Lecture), spaces can be reserved by calling 020 7589 3853.

Passenger lifts at the Royal Albert Hall are located off the ground-floor corridor at Doors 2, 8 and 11.

Booking

Disabled concert-goers (and a companion) receive a 50% discount on all ticket prices (except Arena and Gallery areas) for concerts at the Royal Albert Hall and for Proms Chamber Music concerts at the V&A. To claim this discount, tick the 'Disabled' box at the end of the Booking Form, or call the Access Information Line on 020 7589 3853 if booking by phone (from Friday 15 June).

The Royal Albert Hall has an infra-red system with a number of personal receivers for use with and without hearing aids. To make use of the service, collect a free receiver from the information desk at Door 6.

If you have a guide dog, the best place to sit in the Royal Albert Hall is in a Loggia or Second Tier Box, where your dog may stay with you. If you are sitting elsewhere, stewards will be happy to look after your dog while you enjoy the concert. Please call the Access Information Line on 020 7589 3853 to organise in advance of your visit.

Copies of this Guide are available on audio cassette. Please call 020 7765 3260 to request your copy (priced £4.50).

Braille and computer disc versions are available from RNIB Customer Services on 0845 7023 153. Each set comes in two volumes – Vol. 1 for the listings, Vol. 2 for the articles – priced at £2.25 a volume, £4.50 the set.

Visually impaired patrons are also welcome to use the free infra-red hearing facility (*see above*) to listen in to the broadcast commentary on Radio 3.

Large-print texts and opera librettos can be made available on the night (free upon purchase of a standard concert programme) if ordered not less than five working-days in advance. Large-print concert programmes can be purchased subsequent to any concert, for the same price as the standard programme for the night, by telephoning 020 7765 3260.

Royal Albert Hall Development Update

Audiences at this year's Proms season will see and experience some of the exciting changes now nearing completion as part of the Royal Albert Hall's ongoing development programme (due to finish in 2003), which aims to make much-needed improvements for both public and performers.

The magnificent South Steps approach, the meeting-place for concert queuers, has been restored with re-designed gardens and balustrades from the original 1860s site. Prince Albert's statue on the Monument to the Exhibition of 1851 has been returned to the top of the steps. Underneath them, the vast new space created contains a loading bay giving production crews direct access to the stage, an engineering plant that will supply an air ventilation system in time for the 2002 Proms, new dressing-rooms and workshops.

Inside the Hall, two new bars have already opened at Door 6 (see *page 115*). For your comfort during concerts, there are new Choir seats, while the Grand Tier and Loggia boxes and corridors have also been refurbished.

Work is currently being carried out to create a new Box Office in the South foyer and on the redecoration of the Door 6 entrance, while the foundations have already been laid for the new South Porch, which will contain a shop and a greatly extended, redesigned restaurant. Restoration work is also in progress on the decorative plaster cove around the top of the Gallery, which was damaged and dismantled in the 1940s, while the dome itself is being re-glazed.

Future plans include the creation of two huge new Arena foyers, adding another two bars, and the renovation of the splendid Organ, reinstating it by 2004 to its position as the largest in the United Kingdom.

The Royal Albert Hall is a registered charity and still needs to raise funds for the development. For further information, please contact Sarah Dixon, Head of Development Fundraising on 020 7589 3203 or by e-mail at Fund@royalalberthall.com.

How to Prom

What is Promming?

The popular tradition of Promming is central to the unique and informal atmosphere of the Proms.

Up to 1,000 standing places are available at each Proms concert. The traditionally low prices allow you to enjoy world-class concerts for just £3.00 (£1.50 for Season Ticket-holders).

There are two standing areas: the Arena, which is located directly in front of the stage, and the Gallery, running round the top of the Hall. All spaces are unreserved.

Day Prommers

Over 500 Arena and Gallery tickets (priced £3.00) go on sale to the day Prommers 30 minutes before doors open (one hour before on days when there are Pre-Prom talks). These tickets cannot be booked in advance, so even if all seats have been sold, you always have a good chance of getting in (though early queuing is obviously advisable for the more popular concerts). You must buy your ticket in person.

Buying Your Ticket

Day tickets are available (for cash only) at Door 11 (Arena) and Door 10 (Gallery), not at the Box Office. If in doubt about where to go, Royal Albert Hall stewards will point you in the right direction.

Season Tickets

Dedicated Prommers can save money by purchasing Arena or Gallery Season Tickets covering either the whole Proms season or only the first or second half (*ie* Proms 1–36 or Proms 37–72).

Season Ticket-holders benefit from:
- guaranteed entrance (until 10 minutes before each concert)
- great savings – prices work out at as little as £1.50 per concert
- guaranteed entrance to the Last Night for Whole Season ticket-holders and special access to a reserved allocation of Last Night tickets for Half Season ticket-holders. See *page 119*.

Please note that Season Ticket-holders arriving at the Royal Albert Hall later than 10 minutes before a concert are not guaranteed entry and may be asked, in certain circumstances, to join the day queue.

For further details and prices of Season Tickets, see page 121.

Where to queue

- **Arena Day Queue**
  Enter by Door 11

- **Gallery Day Queue**
  Enter by Door 10

- **Arena Season Queue**
  Enter by Door 2

- **Gallery Season Queue**
  Enter by Door 3

Please note that the South Steps to the Royal Albert Hall have now reopened

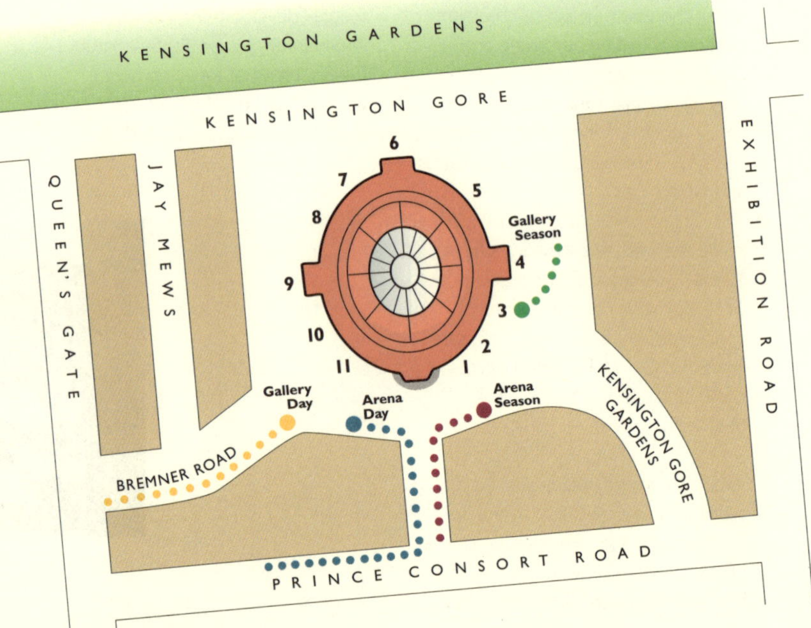

The Last Night

Owing to the huge demand for Last Night tickets, special booking arrangements apply. Your best chance of purchasing tickets for the Last Night of the Proms is through the Priority Booking system

Priority Booking for the Last Night

The Six-Concert Rule

In order to apply for any tickets for the Last Night during the priority booking period (ie before general booking by phone or in person opens on Friday 15 June), you must book for at least six other concerts in the 2001 season.

Book one ticket in the same seating area for at least six other concerts in the 2001 season and you can apply at the same time for a single ticket in the same seating area for the Last Night. For example, book a ticket in the Choir for six concerts, and you can apply for one ticket in the Choir for the Last Night.

Book two or more tickets in the same seating area for at least six other concerts in the 2001 season and you can apply at the same time for a maximum of two tickets in the same seating area for the Last Night (ie. whether you book two or 22 Stalls tickets for six concerts, you can still apply for *only* two Stalls tickets for the Last Night).

Note that, if you book tickets for at least six other concerts but in different seating areas, you will be allocated Last Night seats in the area of the majority of your bookings (unless you specify that lower-priced tickets are desired).

We regret that, if the Last Night is sold out by the time your application is processed, no refunds for other tickets purchased will be payable.

General Booking for the Last Night

Once telephone and personal booking opens (on Friday 15 June), the six-concert rule no longer applies. Note, however, that Last Night tickets have usually sold out by this stage.

Please note that, for all Last Night bookings, only one application (for a maximum of two tickets) can be made per household.

Promming at the Last Night

Day Prommers who have attended six or more other concerts (in either the Arena or the Gallery) can buy one ticket each for the Last Night (priced £3.00) on presentation of their used tickets at the Box Office from 25 July (subject to availability).

Season Ticket-holders Whole Season tickets include admission to the Last Night. A limited allocation of Last Night places is also reserved for Half Season ticket-holders. Holders of First Half Season Tickets can buy one ticket each (priced £3.00) at the Box Office from 25 July (subject to availability). Holders of Second Half Season Tickets can buy tickets in the same way from 23 August.

Queuing Whole Season ticket-holders and other Prommers with Last Night tickets are guaranteed entrance until 10 minutes before the concert. All Prommers (Day or Season) with Last Night tickets should queue at Door 2 (Arena) or Door 3 (Gallery). Please note that the South Steps have now reopened.

Sleeping Out There has long been a tradition of Prommers with Last Night tickets sleeping out overnight to secure the best standing places nearest the front of the Arena. The official queue

will form at 4.00pm on the last Friday of the season at Door 2 (Arena) or Door 10 (Gallery). Those also wishing to attend that night's concert (Prom 72) will be given numbered slips to reserve their places in the queue but must return in person immediately after the end of the concert.

On the Night A small number of standing tickets may be available on the Last Night itself (priced £3.00), one per person, just before the start of the concert. No previous ticket purchases are necessary. If you wish to take a chance, join the queue at Door 11 (Arena) or Door 10 (Gallery).

Bust of Sir Henry Wood on loan from the Royal Academy of Music

Exclusive to Proms Guide Readers

One hundred best seats (priced £70.00) for this year's Last Night of the Proms at the Royal Albert Hall will be allocated by ballot to readers of the *BBC Proms 2001 Guide*. No other ticket purchases are necessary. Only one application (for a maximum of two tickets) may be made per household.

If you would like to apply for tickets by ballot, please complete the official Ballot Form on the back of this slip (photocopies are not acceptable) and send it by post only – to arrive no later than Friday 20 July – to:

BBC Proms Ballot, Box Office, Royal Albert Hall, London SW7 2AP

Note that the Proms Ballot application is completely separate from other Proms booking procedures. Envelopes should be clearly marked 'BBC PROMS BALLOT' and should contain only the official Ballot Form, together with your cheque or card details. If sending a cheque, please also enclose an SAE so that it can be returned to you if your application is unsuccessful.

Successful applicants will be notified by post within two weeks of the ballot, which takes place on Friday 3 August.

BBC PROMS

Title

Initial

Surname

Address

Postcode

Country

Daytime Tel.

Please tick the appropriate boxes

☐ I wish to apply for one ticket (£70.00)

☐ I wish to apply for two tickets (£140.00)

☐ I enclose a cheque made payable to
'Royal Albert Hall' and an SAE.
(Cheques will be returned to unsuccessful
applicants within two weeks of the ballot.)

☐ Please debit my Access/Visa/Amex/
Mastercard/Switch*

Expiry Date   Issue No.*

Signature

Choose your seating area

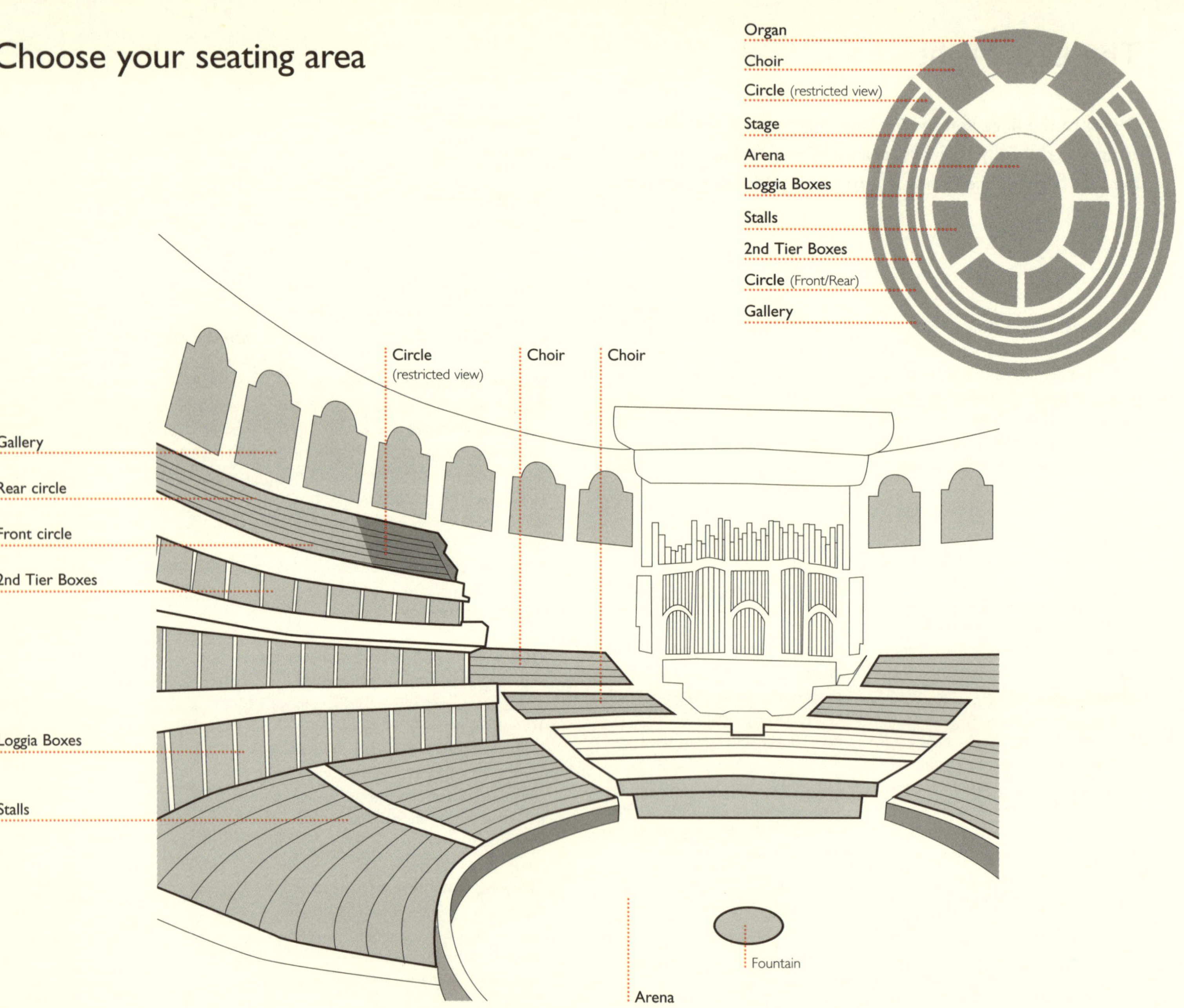

Price Bands for Proms in the Royal Albert Hall

Seats

Each concert falls into one of six different price bands, colour coded for easy reference

	A	B	C	D	E	F
Stalls	£21.50	£27.00	£35.00	£12.00	£70.00	ALL SEATS £10.00 (UNDER-16s £5.00)
Loggia Boxes (8 seats)	£21.50	£27.00	£35.00	£12.00	£70.00	
2nd Tier Boxes (5 seats)	£17.00	£21.50	£30.00	£12.00	£70.00	
Choir	£14.50	£17.50	£23.50	£9.00	£50.00	
Front Circle	£12.50	£14.50	£19.00	£9.00	£50.00	
Rear Circle	£9.00	£10.00	£14.50	£9.00	£40.00	
Circle (restricted view)	£5.00	£6.00	£10.00		£20.00	

Promming

Standing places are available in the Arena and Gallery on the day for £3.00 (see page 118)

Season Tickets	Dates	Arena	Gallery
Whole Season *Proms 1–73*	20 July – 15 September	**£140.00**	**£110.00**

Half Season tickets

First Half *Proms 1–36*	20 July – 17 August	**£80.00**	**£60.00**
Second Half *Proms 37–72*	18 August – 14 September	**£80.00**	**£60.00**

BBC Proms in the Park, London, Saturday 15 September

All tickets £15.00

CBBC Prom in the Park, London, Sunday 16 September

Adults £10.00   **Children £6.00 (3–16 yrs) Under-3s free**

Please note that booking fees apply to all postal, fax and telephone bookings (for details, see Booking Form)

Express booking
Bookings for concerts in price bands B and C will receive priority if at least one concert in price band A is also booked (subject to availability). Tick the box at the end of the Booking Form if your application qualifies.

Disabled concert-goers
Please see page 116 for details of ticket prices, special discounts, access and facilities.

Privately owned seats
A high proportion of boxes, as well as 600 Stalls seats, are privately owned. Unless returned by owners, these seats are not available for sale.

Season tickets
Season tickets can be booked by post (from 21 May) or in person at the Box Office (from 15 June), but not by phone or fax. For postal bookings, complete the special section of the Booking Form (facing page 122). Two passport-sized photographs must be provided with all applications.

Proms Chamber Music
All seats £6.00. For post/fax bookings, complete the Booking Form (facing page 122). Note that Poetry Proms, Composer Portraits and the Proms Lecture are unticketed events, with free admission on a first-come-first-served basis. Pre-Prom Talks are free to ticket-holders for that evening's concert.

How to fill in the Booking Form

• **Choose the concerts** you want to go to and where you want to sit.

• **Enter the number of tickets** you require for each concert under your chosen seating area.

• **Add up the value of tickets** requested and enter the amount in the 'Sub-total' column.

• **To claim any Special Offers** *(see pages 112–113)*, tick the 'discount claimed' column and enter the value of the discount in the 'Discount' column. Subtract the value of the discount from the sub-total and enter the 'Total' at the end of the row.

• **For Under-16 discounts** enter the number of adults within the white area, the number of under-16s within the blue area.

• **For Proms Explorer offers** *(see pages 112–113)* complete the special section of the Booking Form. Note that you must book the same number of tickets in the same seating area for each of your chosen concerts.

• **If the tickets you want are not available**, lower-priced tickets for the same concert will be sent. Please tick the box at the end of the Booking Form if this is *not* acceptable.

• **Tickets cannot be exchanged** for other performances nor refunded except in the event of a cancelled performance.

Booking Queries

If you have any queries about how to fill in the Booking Form, call the Box Office on 020 7589 8212 from 30 April (open 9.00am–9.00pm daily).

Fax Booking

If booking by fax, clearly state your name on all three pages. Please note that fax booking lines are open 24 hours a day. Please do *not* duplicate the form by post.

BOOKING FORM PART 1

Full name of sender (Fax Booking)
Surname D'ANTINO First Name ANNE

Seating Area: please indicate number of seats required

Prom	Date	Time	Price Code	Special Offers See pages 112–13	Stalls	Loggia Boxes (8 seats)	2nd Tier Boxes (5 seats)	Choir	Front Circle	Rear Circle	Circle (restricted view)	Wheelchair space See page 116	Sub-total (£)	Please tick if discount claimed	Discount (£)	Car Parking See page 115	Total (£)	Office Use
1	Friday 20 July	7.30	B						2				29:00				29:00	
2	Saturday 21 July	7.30	B										43:00			✓	49:00	
3	Sunday 22 July	7.30	B		2								43:00			✓	49:00	
4	Monday 23 July	7.30	A	G									24:00	✓	4:00	✓	20:00	
5	Tuesday 24 July	7.30	A		2							X						
6	Wednesday 25 July	7.00	A	→	2													
7	Wednesday 25 July	10.00	D	→, P														
8	Thursday 26 July	7.30	A	P														
9	Friday 27 July	7.30	A					2	2				40:00	✓	10:00	X	30:00	
10	Saturday 28 July	11.00am	F	16														
11	Saturday 28 July	7.30	A	P														
12	Sunday 29 July	7.30	A	P, G														
13	Monday 30 July	7.30	A															
69	Tuesday 11 September	10.00	D	G, 16													35:00	
70	Wednesday 12 September	7.30	C										35:00					
71	Thursday 13 September	7.30	B	G				2										
72	Friday 14 September	7.30	B															
73	Saturday 15 September	7.30	E															

Number of adults   Number of under-16s

Sub-total **212:00**

BOOKING FORM PART I

Full name of sender (Fax Booking) Surname First Name

Seating Area: please indicate number of seats required

Prom	Date	Time	Price Code	Special Offers See pages 112–13	Stalls	Loggia Boxes (8 seats)	2nd Tier Boxes (5 seats)	Choir	Front Circle	Rear Circle	Circle (restricted view)	Wheelchair space See page 116	Sub-total (£)	Please tick if discount claimed	Discount (£)	Car Parking See page 115	Total (£)	Office Use
1	Friday 20 July	7.30	B															
2	Saturday 21 July	7.30	B															
3	Sunday 22 July	7.30	B															
4	Monday 23 July	7.30	A	G														
5	Tuesday 24 July	7.30	A															
6	Wednesday 25 July	7.00	A	→														
7	Wednesday 25 July	10.00	D	←							X							
8	Thursday 26 July	7.30	A	P														
9	Friday 27 July	7.30	A															
10	Saturday 28 July	11.00am	F	16												X		
11	Saturday 28 July	7.30	A															
12	Sunday 29 July	7.30	A	P														
13	Monday 30 July	7.30	A	G														
14	Tuesday 31 July	7.00	A	→ P														
15	Tuesday 31 July	10.00	D	←							X							
16	Wednesday 1 August	7.30	C															
17	Thursday 2 August	7.30	A															
18	Friday 3 August	7.00	A	→														
19	Friday 3 August	10.00	D	←							X							
20	Saturday 4 August	7.30	A	P														
21	Sunday 5 August	2.30	F	G 16												X		
22	Sunday 5 August	8.00	A															
23	Monday 6 August	7.00	A	→														
24	Monday 6 August	10.00	D	←							X							
25	Tuesday 7 August	7.30	A	G														
26	Wednesday 8 August	7.00	A	G														
27	Thursday 9 August	7.30	B															
28	Friday 10 August	7.30	A	P														
29	Saturday 11 August	7.00	A	16														
30	Sunday 12 August	7.30	A	P														
31	Monday 13 August	7.30	A															
32	Tuesday 14 August	7.00	A	→ G														
33	Tuesday 14 August	10.00	D	← G							X							
34	Wednesday 15 August	7.30	A															
35	Thursday 16 August	7.30	C															
36	Friday 17 August	7.30	A															
37	Saturday 18 August	7.00	A	→ G 16														
38	Saturday 18 August	10.00	D	←							X							
39	Sunday 19 August	7.30	A															
40	Monday 20 August	7.00	A	→														
41	Monday 20 August	10.00	D	→							X							
42	Tuesday 21 August	7.30	A	G														
43	Wednesday 22 August	7.30	B															
44	Thursday 23 August	7.00	B	→														
45	Thursday 23 August	10.00	D	←							X							
46	Friday 24 August	7.30	B															
47	Saturday 25 August	7.30	C															
48	Sunday 26 August	7.30	C															
49	Monday 27 August	7.30	C															
50	Tuesday 28 August	7.30	C															
51	Wednesday 29 August	7.00	A	→														
52	Wednesday 29 August	10.00	D	←							X							
53	Thursday 30 August	7.30	B															
54	Friday 31 August	7.00	B	→														
55	Friday 31 August	10.00	D	←							X							
56	Saturday 1 September	7.30	A															
57	Sunday 2 September	7.00	A															
58	Monday 3 September	7.00	B	→ G														
59	Monday 3 September	10.00	D	←							X							
60	Tuesday 4 September	7.30	B															
61	Wednesday 5 September	7.30	B															
62	Thursday 6 September	7.30	A															
63	Friday 7 September	7.00	C	→														
64	Friday 7 September	10.00	D	←							X							

Number of adults — *Number of under-16s*

BBC Proms, Box Office, Royal Albert Hall, Kensington Gore, London SW7 2AP

Fax number:

020 7581 9311

If you fax this booking form, please do not duplicate your order by post

BOOKING FORM PART 2

Full name of sender (Fax Booking) — Surname — First Name

Seating Area: please indicate number of seats required

Prom	Date	Time	Price Code	Special Offers (See pages 112–13)	Stalls	Loggia Boxes (8 seats)	2nd Tier Boxes (5 seats)	Choir	Front Circle	Rear Circle	Circle (restricted view)	Wheelchair space (See page 116)	Sub-total (£)	Please tick if discount claimed	Discount (£)	Car Parking (See page 115)	Total (£)	Office Use
																Total carried over	:	
65	Saturday 8 September	7.30	C										:				:	
66	Sunday 9 September	7.30	B										:				:	
67	Monday 10 September	7.30	A	P									:		:		:	
68	Tuesday 11 September	7.00	C										:				:	
69	Tuesday 11 September	10.00	D							✕			:		:		:	
70	Wednesday 12 September	7.30	C	16									:		:		:	
71	Thursday 13 September	7.30	B										:				:	
72	Friday 14 September	7.30	B	G									:		:		:	
73	Saturday 15 September	7.30	E										:				:	

Sub-total :

Proms Explorer (E)

See page 112

Note that you must book the same number of tickets in the same seating area for each concert.
Programme vouchers will be posted with your tickets.

	Date	Time	Price Code	Stalls	Front Circle	Rear Circle	Wheelchair space (See page 116)	Car Parking (See page 115)	Total (£)
4	Monday 23 July	7.30	A						:
9	Friday 27 July	7.30	A						:
18	Friday 3 August	7.00	A						:
27	Thursday 9 August	7.30	B						:
32	Tuesday 14 August	7.00	A						:
36	Friday 17 August	7.30	A						:
42	Tuesday 21 August	7.30	A						:
54	Friday 31 August	7.00	B						:
60	Tuesday 4 September	7.30	B						:
72	Friday 14 September	7.30	B						:

Sub-total before discount		:
I've booked for 3 or 4 concerts and claim my 10% discount	−	:
I've booked for 5 concerts and claim my 15% discount	−	:
I've booked for 5 concerts and claim my free Late Night Prom (ticked in the list below)		

19	Friday 3 August	10.00	
33	Tuesday 14 August	10.00	FREE
55	Friday 31 August	10.00	

Sub-total :

Proms Chamber Music — Mondays at 1.00pm (all tickets £6.00)

See pages 110–111

		Number of tickets	Total (£)			Number of tickets	Total (£)
PCM 1	23 July		:	PCM 5	20 August		:
PCM 2	30 July		:	PCM 6	27 August		:
PCM 3	6 August		:	PCM 7	3 September		:
PCM 4	13 August		:	PCM 8	10 September		:
	Total to carry over	:				**Sub-total**	:

Season Tickets — See page 118

		Arena	Gallery	Number of tickets Arena	Gallery
Whole Season	Proms 1–73 (Friday 20 July – Saturday 15 September)	£140.00	£110.00		
First Half	Proms 1–36 (Friday 20 July – Friday 17 August)	£80.00	£60.00		
Second Half	Proms 37–72 (Saturday 18 August – Friday 14 September)	£80.00	£60.00		

☐ Two passport-sized photographs enclosed.

Sub-total : :

Sum of sub-totals £ : **+ Booking Fee** £ 2:00 **= Parts 1&2 Total** £ :

BOOKING FORM PART 3

Full name of sender (Fax Booking)   Surname   First Name

BBC Proms in the Park, London, Saturday 15 September

See page 109

All tickets £15.00 plus £1.35 booking fee per ticket. Indicate number required below.

	Number of tickets required		Total (£)
Ticket plus booking fee: £15.00 + £1.35 = £16.35	@ £16.35 each	**Sub-total**	:

CBBC Prom in the Park, London, Sunday 16 September

See page 109

Adults: £10.00 plus £1.25 booking fee per ticket. Children (3–16 years): £6.00 plus £1.00 booking fee per ticket. Under-3s free. Indicate number required below.

	Number of tickets required	Total (£)
Adult ticket plus booking fee: £10.00 + £1.25 = £11.25	@ £11.25 each	:
Child ticket plus booking fee: £6.00 + £1.00 = £7.00	@ £7.00 each	:
	Sub-total	:

Part 3 Total   £   :

Sum of totals

Total from Parts 1&2   £   :   **+**   Total from Part 3   £   :   **= Grand Total**   £   :

(BLOCK CAPITALS PLEASE)

Title   Initial   Surname

Address

Country   Postcode

Daytime telephone   Evening telephone

If you know your Royal Albert Hall account number please write it here

Payment by cheque

☐ I enclose a cheque made payable to 'Royal Albert Hall'. (Please leave cheques open, with an upper limit.)

Payment by credit card/debit card

Please debit my Access/Visa/American Express/Mastercard/Switch* account for: £   :

My card number is: Expiry Date: Issue No.*

Signature

☐ I claim the special discount for disabled concert-goers (see page 116).

☐ My ticket order qualifies as an Express booking (see page 121).

☐ Do not send lower-priced tickets (see page 124).

☐ Order sent by fax. (Please send all three pages.)

☐ **BBC Proms is part of the BBC. The BBC** would like to contact you in future with information about **BBC Proms** and other relevant **BBC** services, events and programmes. If you would like to receive this information please tick here.

☐ **The BBC Proms take place at the Royal Albert Hall. If you would like the Royal Albert Hall to contact you in future with information about events and other developments at the Royal Albert Hall, please tick here.**

Please note that booking fees are added to cover postage and administration. When making your booking, you will automatically be sent a personal account number to link in with the RAH computerised system. Please quote this number in all future transactions. Tickets will be delivered within 28 days.

BBC Proms, Box Office, Royal Albert Hall, Kensington Gore, London SW7 2AP

Fax number:

020 7581 9311

If you fax this booking form, please do not duplicate your order by post

My nights with the stars

Music critic and broadcaster **Rob Cowan** explains
why he enjoys spending his Last Nights out of doors

LEFT
José Carreras makes his
Proms debut in Hyde Park

BELOW
Terry Wogan returns to Hyde
Park to host what he swears
his listeners call 'Prawns in the
Park' or 'Prams in the Dark'.
'Either way,' he says, 'I look
forward to it enormously each
year – 40,000 people in all
weathers and a wonderful
time is had by all'

The traditional Last Night crowd is a fired-up community singing its heart out, a coming-together with no hint of dissent. Flags, streamers and stamping feet set the scene, both inside the Royal Albert Hall and on our TV screens. But turn to Hyde Park, and Heathrow-bound jets replace the Hall's acoustical flying saucers, banners wave in counterpoint with trees and, on a good day, the sun and moon serve as nature's spotlights. A West End parkland becomes a heavily populated arena with chattering queues, mounted police in peaceful attendance and music issuing from lofty loudspeakers. Even now I can recall how,

at the first Proms in the Park in 1996, a long-necked crane with satellite discs for eyes gazed from the edge of the festival site towards the Albert Memorial a mile or so away. Streams of promenaders journey from one venue to the other, passing the Serpentine, sweat-banded joggers, kids playing ball games and clumps of munching picnickers.

With fast-food trucks marking the site perimeter, the grass in front of the huge concave stage starts to fill with people from as early as 4.00pm. Voice tests, video tests, sundry announcements and the heady confusion as visitors bag places to settle down, all add to the

Proms in the Park

This year, Proms in the Park events are being held in more venues around the UK than ever before, giving even more people the chance to share in the unique atmosphere that traditionally surrounds the Last Night of the Proms. With Terry Wogan presiding for the sixth year running over the open-air festivities in London's Hyde Park, and simultaneous celebrations taking place in spectacular outdoor locations in Liverpool, Gateshead and St Austell, Cornwall (at the newly opened Eden

Project), this year's Last Night party should be the biggest yet. And with celebrity appearances by the likes of José Carreras and Jools Holland (Hyde Park), Kathryn Tickell (Gateshead) and former Young Musician of the Year, Natalie Clein (St Austell), it should be a night of stars all round.

For further details and booking information,
see page 109

**RENAULT – Official sponsor
of Proms in the Park, London,
and CBBC Prom in the Park**

'I'm very proud that I am finally making my first appearance at the Proms. This may be an easy-going kind of an event, but for me it's as important as any first night at Covent Garden'
José Carreras

Marcin Tyszka (Carreras)

atmosphere. Strolling between the seated parties, past baskets and bottles, cheeses and canapés, you can eavesdrop on communal enthusiasms. Nothing can dampen people's spirits, not even a passing shower. On-stage entertainment starts at around 5.30pm, but as the evening draws closer and the excitement builds, the lawn transforms into a vast field of eager faces. Look back across the crowd stretching away towards Marble Arch and you can hardly believe that so many people have come together in so short a time. The sense of community is almost tangible.

First on stage is the more popular fare, the songs that everyone knows. Then, for the main concert, there are the to-ings and fro-ings between Park and Hall, with key performers beamed up from the 'big indoors' onto two huge video screens. As darkness descends, candles, lanterns and torches set the scene for a secular vigil, the music interspersed with storms of applause. And of course there's the last lap, the Union Jacks, whistles, hooters and hats, the heckling laughter and pockets of dancing, the sense of all us Prommers in different parks and spaces across the country all being linked in one giant community party. Last year, I was lucky enough to be inside the Hall, but almost felt envious of everyone outside.

If you've ever sat at home, watching the Last Night on TV, and suspected that being in the Hall might be fun, you really ought to try the Park. Listening and laughing under a night sky seems to bring out the child in all of us. A mighty sing-song and joining-of-arms makes even the most crowded football match seem tepid by comparison. So, with more Proms in the Park events programmed this year than ever before, do yourself a favour and join this nationwide celebration of music's power to exhilarate and reconcile.

C B B C Prom in the Park

Are you ready to play? If so, why not take the children along to Hyde Park on Sunday 16 September, the day after the Last Night of the Proms, for the second ever CBBC Prom in the Park – a fun-filled family afternoon featuring live appearances by those two popular foursomes Jake, Fizz, Milo and Bella (aka The Tweenies), and Ben, Mark, Christian and Paul (aka a1, the A-team band voted Best Newcomers at the Brits)? Following the success of the 1999 event, in which Mr Blobby made his surprise conducting debut and S Club 7 vied with the *1812*, Blue Peter's Matt Baker and Simon Thomas, with Faye Tozer from Steps, will host 2001's show live on stage. There'll be guest appearances by other stars and friends from CBBC. Plus there's Rumon Gamba to conduct the BBC Philharmonic. And if they're not ready to play, no one is!

For further details and booking information, see page 109

ABOVE
Meet the A-team, bestselling boy band a1; get ready to play with The Tweenies; and prepare to step out with Faye

LEFT
Your hosts for this year's CBBC Prom in the Park: Matt Baker and Simon Thomas from *Blue Peter*

For *further details and booking information, see page 109*

Poetry Proms Recorded for later broadcast on BBC Radio 3

Jo Shapcott, last year's Proms Poet-in-Residence, looks back on the first season of Poetry Proms

In retrospect, it's amazing that Poetry Proms had never been done before. Once we started, it seemed so obvious. Proms audiences are used to poetry – set to music, of course – but they are used to the concentration of words and ideas.

Sitting and listening, intently but informally, is the essence of Prom-going. It's also how poets like their work to be heard. The Serpentine Gallery too – or the grass outside it – has just the right atmosphere. It is home to the newest and most daring art without being off-putting. Holding the readings there meant that the audience could experience the best of three art forms in an evening without getting cultural indigestion.

The context was important for us poets too. By commissioning a new piece from each writer, and linking it with the theme of the evening's concert, we were working in the best tradition of the Proms. These were to be no ordinary readings. They were to place poetry outside the music but firmly connected to it. Usually in a concert series the words are necessarily subordinate to the music (frequently barely heard or unintelligible – depending on who's set them). Here they were presented in their own right, and the music could take over in the evening from where we left off.

We were lucky for the first season to have a good cross-section of poets writing in English now. There were some who have the same star status as

ABOVE
Jo Shapcott: last year's Proms Poet-in-Residence returns this year to present a second series of Poetry Proms

BELOW
The Serpentine Gallery, where art and poetry meet

RIGHT
Rachel Whiteread's *Table and Chair (Clear)*, one of the works on show at The Serpentine during the Proms season

Anthony D'Offay Gallery (Whiteread)

Friday 20 July, 6.00pm–c6.45pm
Friday 3 August, 5.30pm–c6.15pm
Friday 17 August, 6.00pm–c6.45pm
Friday 31 August, 5.30pm–c6.15pm
Serpentine Gallery, Kensington Gardens

Following the success of last year's inaugural Poetry Proms, the BBC presents a second series of fortnightly pre-concert poetry readings at the Serpentine Gallery.

Situated in the heart of Kensington Gardens in a 1934 tea pavilion, the gallery was founded in 1970 and is now one of London's best-loved exhibition sites for modern and contemporary art.

Each of the four 45-minute events will feature four poets who have been commissioned to write a poem focusing on this year's Proms themes: exile and pastoral. The events will be presented by Jo Shapcott, last year's Poet-in-Residence, while guest poets will include Michael Longley, Selima Hill, Lavinia Greenlaw, Michael Donaghy, Kate Clanchy, Ken Smith, Kathleen Jamie, David Harsent (librettist of Birtwistle's 1991 opera *Gawain*) and Michael Symmons Roberts (who has written the text for James MacMillan's new BBC commission, *Birds of Rhiannon*, being premiered in Prom 8).

This year's Poet-in-Residence will be the Australian-born Peter Porter, who came to Britain 50 years ago. It has been written of him that he is 'vehement, jokey, humane, erudite – he does elegy, fantasy, meditations on death, illness, art, music, great European cities, Australian landscape, sex and the over-40s'.

Poetry Proms will be recorded and broadcast by Radio 3 as interval features during each Tuesday's Prom

Admission to Poetry Proms is free, but there is limited availability. It will not be possible to admit latecomers.

The Serpentine Gallery is open daily (10.00am–6.00pm); admission is free. Poetry Proms audiences can also visit the current exhibition of sculptures by Rachel Whiteread (20 June–5 August).

the conductors and soloists appearing in the Albert Hall, like the Poet Laureate, Andrew Motion, or Ursula Fanthorpe. Then there were those who are seen as among the best of their generation, like Jackie Kay, Simon Armitage, Maura Dooley and George Szirtes. We had 16 poets in all, and they covered the spectrum just as comprehensively as the composers across the road.

Poetry is practised more than it is read, listened to more than it is bought. Like contemporary composers, our reputations are often rather higher than our sales figures. So one of the most valuable things about last year's Poetry Proms was the publication of the commissioned poems in a Radio 3 booklet a couple of weeks before the end of the season. This was given out free with the programme for selected concerts. Theoretically, if every seat had been sold and everyone in the audience had bought a programme, over 50,000 people would have gone home with a book of poems. It's the sort of readership usually only enjoyed by whodunit writers.

This year, the poets will be back: a new selection but just as varied and capable of taking the Prom-goer into new areas of enjoyment and exploration. Not everybody will like every poem, and not every poem can promise to be a revelation. But, collectively, we can promise to be just as intriguing as those who have an orchestra to play with.

Performing Art Recorded for later broadcast on BBC Radio 3

Christopher Cook reveals how art objects find their musical match at the V&A

It's a dark February afternoon. The staff at the V&A are about to shut up shop on one of the world's greatest collections of the decorative arts. And here am I and Edward Blakeman, who produces the Proms Chamber Music concerts at the Victoria and Albert Museum, being given a private view of selected treasures from the collection by Rowan Watson, the curator responsible for the art featured in this year's Performing Art series.

We look at a piano with panels painted by Burne-Jones – a possible contender for an all-Schubert recital. Difficult though, we agree, for an audience in the Lecture Theatre to see them in all their pre-Raphaelite glory.

We walk on in pursuit of the 'Pastoral', one of this year's Proms themes. And, while hunting down posters designed by Paul Nash and Graham Sutherland for the Shell Oil Company in the years between the wars ('Go Well, Go Shell'), we are wonderfully distracted by an image from the 1950s with cathedral-like woods, a large sheep and a quotation from Milton. It's London Underground encouraging city-dwellers to refresh their lungs out in the green belt.

As we climb up into the Aladdin's cave that is the museum's new glass gallery, we unanimously applaud one art performer for this summer's season. *Sea Form* by the contemporary American glass-maker Dale Chihuly. So which recital will it accompany? That's for you to find out in August.

The idea is the same as it's been over the past two years in which Performing Art has been a curtain-raiser for lunchtime music-making at the V&A during the Proms. A member of the curatorial staff joins me in the Lecture Theatre to talk about an item from the collection that casts light on the music that we're about to hear. (Audiences at home get their chance to 'hear' the art during the interval of the following Thursday's Prom; the recital itself is repeated the Sunday after.)

Sometimes the light cast is bright and direct, and sometimes it throws all

ABOVE

The Victoria & Albert Museum: home to this year's Performing Art talks, Proms Chamber Music recitals, Proms Composer Portraits, Verdi Study Event and the BBC Proms Lecture

BELOW

Sea Form by Dale Chihuly: one of the art objects that Christopher Cook has chosen from the V&A collection as the subject for a Performing Art talk. But which recital will it accompany?

V&A London

manner of interesting shadows. Last year an American streamlined radio in the shape of a bullet, made by the Fada Company in 1940, preceded the Nash Ensemble playing music by Copland, one of Proms 2000's featured composers. A direct connection: an American radio receiver for a composer who transmits a unique version of America.

Where, though, was the link between a terracotta table sculpture of the Three Graces by Joseph Nollekens – that great English sculptor who straddled the 18th and 19th centuries – and Steven Osborne and Paul Lewis playing György Kurtág's transcriptions from Bach? The answer: both artists, composer and sculptor, are reworking ideas from the past – the music of Bach, and the traditional ways in which the Three Graces have been represented since classical antiquity.

So, 12 months on, we're back in the museum trying to match a new set of musicians and themes to works of art. This year there's Finzi and Schoenberg … Well, England and Vienna are easy to find in the V&A – both excelled at the decorative arts at the turn of the 19th century. As for this season's themes, you tumble across the 'Pastoral' in unexpected places in this great collection. But 'Exile'? Maybe that's what most museums are about, filled as they are with works of art that have left home, most often of their own free will but sometimes only after staring into the muzzle of a musket.

For details of Performing Art and Proms Chamber Music, see pages 110–111

Proms Composer Portraits Broadcast live on BBC Radio 3

Proms Composer Portraits change venue this year to join Proms Chamber Music and Performing Art at the Victoria & Albert Museum

Each of the four early-evening events features chamber music by a leading living composer who has a major new work being performed at the Proms on – or close to – the day of his Composer Portrait.

All Proms Composer Portraits are at 6.00pm in the Lecture Theatre at the V&A. Admission is free, but there is limited availability. Latecomers will not be admitted until a suitable break in the performance.

Thursday 26 July, 6.00pm
James MacMillan in conversation with **Andrew McGregor**

For Ian (solo piano)	3'
London premiere	
Piano Sonata	14'
Cumnock Fair, for piano and string quintet	10'

Performers to be announced

Saturday 4 August, 6.00pm
Sir John Tavener in conversation with **Sarah Walker**

The Child Lived, for soprano and cello	7'
Ieró Óniro, for soprano and ensemble	15'
Samaveda, for soprano, flute and tampura	5'

Performers to be announced

Monday 13 August, 6.00pm
Esa-Pekka Salonen in conversation with **Sarah Walker**

Concert Étude, for solo horn	6'
Second Meeting, for oboe and piano	11'
Yta II, for solo piano	6'

Musicians from the Royal Academy of Music

Thursday 6 September, 6.00pm
John Adams in conversation with **Andrew McGregor**

Road Movies, for violin and piano	15'
John's Book of Alleged Dances for string quartet and tape (selection)	13'

Musicians from the Guildhall School of Music & Drama

See also 'New Music', pages 70–77

ABOVE
Sarah Walker

BELOW
Andrew McGregor

The BBC Proms Lecture
Sunday 19 August, 5.30–c6.30pm
Lecture Theatre, Victoria & Albert Museum
Broadcast live on BBC Radio 3

Details to be announced

Admission is free, but there is limited availability. Latecomers will not be admitted.

Pre-Prom Talks

Our expanded series of Pre-Prom Talks includes meet-the-player events, a Verdi afternoon, and informal introductions to the music you're about to hear, given by composers, performers and other musical experts. **Admission is free to ticket-holders for the following Prom**

Key to venues
RAH • Royal Albert Hall (Auditorium); enter by Door 6
IC • Imperial College (Mechanical Engineering Lecture Theatre 220)
V&A • Victoria & Albert Museum (Lecture Theatre); enter from Exhibition Road

Saturday 21 July, 6.00pm
RAH • William Christie talks to Nicholas Kenyon about Handel

Sunday 22 July, 3.30–6.00pm
V&A • Verdi Study Event, chaired by Roger Parker. Speakers include Pierluigi Petrobelli, Director of the Verdi Institute. *Limited availability; free tickets at Exhibition Road entrance from 2.45pm*

Wednesday 25 July, 5.30pm
IC • Composer Christopher Rouse and pianist Emanuel Ax talk with Radio 3's Rob Cowan

Friday 27 July, 6.00pm
RAH • Richard Hickox talks about Rubbra to Paul Guinery

Sunday 29 July, 6.00pm
RAH • Composer Sally Beamish talks to Lynne Walker about her Proms commission, *Knotgrass Elegy*

Tuesday 31 July, 5.30pm
IC • Stuart MacRae discusses his Proms commission with Richard Stilgoe and Edward Blakeman

Thursday 2 August, 6.00pm
RAH • Geoffrey Chew introduces Kurt Weill's early opera *Royal Palace*

Monday 6 August, 5.30pm
IC • Composer Ian Wilson discusses his BBC commission *Man-o'-War* with Colin Riley

Wednesday 8 August, 5.30pm
RAH • David Wyn Jones on Haydn and Eszterháza

Thursday 9 August, 6.00pm
RAH • Stephen Johnson on Grieg's incidental music for Ibsen's *Peer Gynt*

Friday 10 August, 6.00pm
RAH • Composer Poul Ruders talks to Radio 3 presenter Chris de Souza about his new double percussion concerto, *Studium*

Sunday 12 August, 6.00pm
RAH • Composer Tobias Picker and cellist Paul Watkins discuss the night's new concerto

Tuesday 14 August, 5.30pm
IC • Details to be announced

Thursday 16 August, 6.00pm
RAH • Christopher Hailey introduces Beethoven's *Fidelio*

Monday 20 August, 5.30pm
IC • Christopher Hailey on Proms featured composer, Arnold Schoenberg

Thursday 23 August, 5.30pm
IC • John Evans, Radio 3's Head of Music Programmes and Britten scholar, talks about Britten's time in America

Saturday 25 August, 6.00pm
RAH • Members of the Boston Symphony Orchestra talk to Sue Knussen

Wednesday 29 August, 5.30pm
IC • Composer/conductor Pierre Boulez talks to Nicholas Kenyon

Thursday 30 August, 6.00pm
RAH • The conductor Herbert Blomstedt and Andreas Schültz, General Manager of the Leipzig Gewandhaus Orchestra, talk to Christopher Cook

Sunday 2 September, 5.30pm
RAH • Julian Philips discusses his Proms commission, *Out of Light*, with Radio 3's Edward Seckerson

Saturday 8 September, 6.00pm
RAH • Composer Augusta Read Thomas introduces her *Aurora*

Monday 10 September, 6.00pm
RAH • Alexander Goehr discusses his *second musical offering* with Christopher Cook

Audience Forum
Sunday 9 September, 5.45–c6.30pm
Auditorium, Royal Albert Hall. An opportunity to share your views on the BBC Proms with representatives from the BBC and the Royal Albert Hall

Giuseppe Verdi

❖ 1813 – 1901 ❖

Casa Ricordi, original publisher of all the great Italian opera composers, has been committed for the last twenty-five years to producing critical or urtext editions of the operas. The Verdi critical edition is produced in collaboration with the University of Chicago Press, Rossini with Fondazione Rossini and Donizetti with the Comune di Bergamo.

Ricordi also publishes 20th and 21st century music from Respighi through Nono, Maderna, Grisey and Donatoni to today's composers such as Sciarrino, Francesconi, Battistelli, Guo Wenjing, Liza Lim, not forgetting the operas of Berio.

RICORDI

Tel: 020 7384 8195 · **Fax:** 020 7371 7270
Miranda.Jackson@bmg.co.uk

Director **Janet Ritterman**
MMus, PhD, DUniv, FRNCM,
HonGSMD, HonRAM

Shaping *your* musical future

One of the world's leading conservatoires the Royal College of Music lies at the centre of South Kensington's cultural family. Situated behind the Royal Albert Hall the RCM trains musicians to the highest international level offering:

- Undergraduate degrees

- Postgraduate programmes to doctoral level

- Extensive performing opportunities with over 250 concerts every year

- Internationally significant research collections of manuscripts, instruments, portraits and programmes

- Research projects in music performance, musicology, organology and psychology of music

- futures@rcm: Woodhouse Centre-a career development centre offering support and advice to students for a successful career

- Hall of Residence

Royal College of Music   tel: 020 7589 3643
Prince Consort Road   fax:020 7589 7740
London SW7 2BS   www.rcm.ac.uk

DURHAM CATHEDRAL CHOIR

Join one of England's finest choirs in the dramatic Cathedral City of Durham

Choristers Voice trials for boys aged 7 to 9 are held each May and November. The Cathedral substantially subsidises their education and boarding fees.

The Headmaster, Stephen Drew, The Chorister School
Durham DH1 3EL Tel: 0191 384 2935
email: head@choristers.durham.sch.uk
www.choristers.durham.sch.uk

Choral Scholars The Cathedral offers major scholarships and performance tuition for places held with the University of Durham. Applications to be made normally by December.

The Organist, James Lancelot, 6 The College
Durham DH1 3EQ Tel: 0191 386 4766
email: joyce.newton@durhamcathedral.co.uk
www.durhamcathedral.co.uk

ST PAUL'S GIRLS' SCHOOL

Brook Green Hammersmith
London W6 7BS

An independent day school for girls aged 11-18, we offer academic and music scholarships and bursary awards. Open Days will be held during October 2001.

MUSIC SCHOLARSHIPS for entry to the school in September 2002 are offered to girls at 11+ and 16+ who have satisfied our academic entry requirements. The closing dates for applications are 31 October 2001 (16+) and 30 November 2001 (11+).

For further information please contact the Registrar, Mrs Lindy Hayward on 020 7605 4882

ST MARY'S SCHOOL, CALNE
Wiltshire SN11 0DF

Telephone: 01249 857200
Facsimile: 01249 857207
Email: sms@stmaryscalne.wilts.sch.uk
Website: www.stmaryscalne.wilts.sch.uk

Independent boarding and day school for 300 girls aged 11-18 with a strong academic tradition, excellent pastoral care and tutor system and a comprehensive extra-curricular activities programme.

- **Two Music scholarships** of one-third fees and **several Music bursaries** in the form of free tuition in one or more instruments are available to young musicians joining the school at the age of 11, 12 or 13.
- **One Sixth Form Music Scholarship** of one-third fees is also available and may be awarded to an external or internal applicant.
- Auditions are held in January for girls entering the school at 11, 12 or 13 and in November for Sixth Form entry.
- Full details are available from the Director of Music, Keith Abrams, who will be pleased to give advice at any stage.

For a prospectus please contact the Registrar.
The school has charity status A309482

DULWICH COLLEGE

DIRECTOR OF MUSIC: MICHAEL ASHCROFT

Come and find out why many professional musicians send their sons to Dulwich College

Dulwich College is a viable alternative to the specialist music school. Instrumental and Choral Scholarships are available. If you would like a prospectus, a video and further information, contact The Music Department, Dulwich College, London SE21 7LD or telephone 020 8299 9258.

Charity No.312755 Dulwich College exists to provide education for children

Broadcasts

Arena to Gallery: 'We're on the air!'

Stephen Pollard explains how the BBC brings the Proms
to a wider audience – and wider still – via radio, television
and the internet

We all know that Radio 3 broadcasts every single Prom live. It's one of the BBC's proudest boasts. But have you ever wondered what that entails? Stick up a few microphones, plonk a presenter in the hall and flick a couple of switches, perhaps? Hardly. With over 70 concerts on successive nights – and often more than one concert on the same day – relaying the Proms on radio alone is an astonishing feat of broadcasting, and plans for this year's season were under way even before last year's finished.

But the Proms are not, of course, broadcast just on Radio 3. This year, more Proms than ever are being televised: five and a half Proms are being shown live on BBC2, with BBC1 covering the famous second half (of the Last Night, that is) as well as recording another four concerts, one of them based on the Nation's Favourite Classical Music, specially designed for BBC 1. Plus, for the first time ever, a week of Proms will be going out live on the BBC's digital TV channel, BBC Knowledge. Add the fact that every concert is now also streamed live via the BBC Proms website (at www.bbc.co.uk/proms),

and you can begin to see the scale of the enterprise.

Detailed planning begins in February, with the first of a series of meetings chaired by Radio 3's Executive Producer, Edward Blakeman. Also present are the Artistic Administrator and Concerts Administrator of the Proms, the Executive Producer for Classical Music on Television, the Senior Studio Manager, the Senior Outside Broadcast Sound Supervisor and the Chief Outside Broadcast Engineer. As Blakeman puts it: 'It's a very long meeting! We go through every concert, talking through the requirements and possible problems – or challenges! On days when there are two Proms, the sheer comings and goings can be a logistical brain-teaser.'

Blakeman then draws up a rota, assigning a producer to each concert. The producer's job is to take charge of the broadcast, assuring the quality of the sound that comes into our homes and working with the presenter for the evening on the overall presentation.

First Nights, nowadays, are always on a Friday. The previous Monday morning, Blakeman and his team move

ABOVE

Edward Blakeman, Radio 3's Executive Producer for the Proms, and Christopher Cook, one of the presentation team (as well as host of the weekly Performing Art talks), discuss the script for one of last year's Proms broadcasts

ABOVE
'We are now going over to the Queen's Hall': a 1930s *Radio Times* cartoon by Arthur Watts. Until its destruction in a German air raid in 1941, the original home of the Proms was at the Queen's Hall, just a few steps away from Broadcasting House and All Souls, Langham Place

BOTTOM RIGHT
Radio 3's DSV (Digital Sound Vehicle) parked outside the Royal Albert Hall during a recent Proms season (plus a detail of its mixing-desk)

in to the hall to rig up the array of microphones that hang from the roof and capture the basic sound-image. These are augmented with microphones on stage for the differing needs of particular concerts. 'The alchemy', says Blakeman, 'consists in taking this collection of mikes and mixing their output into the music you receive at home. It should all sound as vivid as actually being in the Royal Albert Hall.'

That is a far from straightforward task. If you've ever been to the Proms, you've probably noticed a BBC van parked permanently outside Door 11. That is the hub of the whole operation. The microphones feed the sound into junction-boxes deep in the bowels of the Royal Albert Hall, from which it then passes, via a series of cables that come up through the pavement outside Door 11, into the BBC van, known as the DSV (Digital Sound Vehicle). Inside the DSV sits a studio manager, who balances the input he gets from the microphones, before sending it back into the hall. It's there received by another studio manager and the producer, who sit inside the familiar glass-fronted BBC box (Loggia 2) at the left-hand side of the stage. They then mix the musical feed with the words of the presenter – seated just in front of the BBC box – and the combined music-speech mix is then sent back to Door 11, from where it leaves South Kensington, via a satellite dish on top of the Albert Hall, *en route* to a receiver at Broadcasting House – and thence to radio listeners at home or on the move.

Add TV to the equation, and the picture gets more complicated still. For television does not just add visuals to the music, it requires an entirely different approach – including its own separate sound-mix, balanced to reflect TV's tendency to spotlight individual players or sections on screen.

Now that TV Classical Music has been brought under the wing of the BBC's new multi-media Radio and Music Division, under Proms Director Nicholas Kenyon, the planning of the Proms and their televising is increasingly integrated. Peter Maniura, Head of TV Classical Music, discusses with the relevant Controllers the choices from the season, and by March, Oliver Macfarlane, the Executive Producer for Classical Music on Television, is already assigning a director to each of the chosen concerts and working out what equipment will be needed. The production and technical team (over 30 in all) then gets to work on the nitty-gritty – planning camera shots, preparing scripts and interval packages, even deciding which seats can't be sold because they'll have cameras on them. The interval packages, in particular, require careful thought. As Macfarlane explains: 'Since Radio 3 and BBC2 often share them, we have to ensure that anything we show on TV is equally intelligible to radio listeners.'

The Last Night, naturally, is in a league of its own – especially since the launch of Proms in the Park in 1996. 'This year we will have cameras in Hyde Park, Liverpool, Gateshead and the

Eden Project in Cornwall – as well as in the Albert Hall itself, of course.'

So much for traditional broadcasting media. But there's now an extra tool that you can use to access the Proms, and which last year was used by around 90,000 people a week: the internet. www.bbc.co.uk/proms is there to bring a new dimension to the Proms – offering regularly updated concert listings, background information, booking details, features and, in the off-season months, reviews and reminders of the previous year's highlights. Leigh Aspin, the Online Producer, describes it as 'an accessible gateway to the Proms. We cater for everyone,' he explains, 'from the enthusiast who needs quick access to information, to the novice who might

Lynda Stone (bottom right)

want to know where to park or if there's a dress code – there isn't! – or even just what the Proms are all about.'

Every week during the season Aspin sends out an e-mail newsletter with highlights, previews, audio clips and artist profiles. There's also a 'fun and games' section, featuring four competitions each season with Proms tickets as prizes, and a positively addictive children's composing game, while the virtual tour of the Royal Albert Hall, shot with a fish-eye lens, is tremendous fun – especially the conductor's-eye views from the podium. Added to all that, of course, every single Prom is streamed live via the site – so, even if you don't have access to BBC radio or TV, you can listen to the Proms wherever in the world you might be.

All broadcast details were correct at the time of going to press. For current schedules, consult 'Radio Times' or other listings publications.

Proms Online

Visit the Proms website at
www.bbc.co.uk/proms

Stephanie Hughes

Stephanie Hughes is now one of the most familiar faces (and voices) of the Proms. The first woman to present the Last Night on TV (a feat she'll repeat this year), she has presented dozens more Proms on both radio and television. And yet, she says, it remains her dream job:

'I still can't believe that I am actually a part of these famous concerts. Every year I do many other concerts from all sorts of other places, but there's nowhere else on earth like the Albert Hall. This year I'll be presenting six concerts on radio and three on TV, as well as the eight V&A chamber music concerts. It's a big commitment, but it's also the best job in the world.'

One of the things Stephanie most values about the Proms is their variety – and not just the music. 'There isn't a typical listener; that's one of the many wonderful things about the Proms. Some people come in their gym shoes and tracksuit, others in their finery, drinking champagne. There's nothing else like that in the world.'

When she is presenting, her days start at about 10.00am. 'For radio, I

Proms on BBC RADIO 3 **BBC RADIO 3** 90-93 FM

Every Prom is broadcast live on BBC Radio 3 and many can be heard again on weekday afternoons at 2.00pm.

Proms Chamber Music concerts and Proms Composer Portraits are all broadcast live, while Poetry Proms and Performing Art talks are broadcast as interval features during Tuesday and Thursday evening Proms respectively.

Both *Morning on 3* (daily, 6.00-9.00am) and *In Tune* (weekdays, 5.00pm) carry updates on the season's progress, while *Festival Music Matters* (Sundays, 12.15pm) includes coverage of the Proms alongside other summer music festivals worldwide.

Listen out too for the following special Proms-related programming:

Discovering Music (Sundays, 4.00pm)

22 July	Gerard McBurney on Schubert: String Quintet in C major
29 July	Stephen Johnson on Strauss: Four Last Songs
5 August	Roger Nichols on Bartók: String Quartet No. 6
12 August	Gerard McBurney on Ives: Three Places in New England
19 August	Chris de Souza on Beethoven: 'Emperor' Concerto
26 August	Gerard McBurney on Shostakovich: Symphony No. 5
2 September	Roger Nichols on Mozart: Piano Concerto No. 25 in C major, K503
9 September	Anthony Payne on Schubert: Piano Trio in B flat major, D898

Proms Documentaries (Sundays, 5.45pm)

22 July	Pastoral Sympathies
29 July	Universal Harmonies
5 August	'Music Ho!' Revisited
12 August	Songs in a Strange Land
19 August	The BBC Proms Lecture
26 August	The Schoenberg Factor
2 September	Barenboim: Master Musician
9 September	Il maestro Verdi!

have a basic script in advance, but the real work begins when I go to the hall for the morning rehearsal. I try to capture the colour, watching the conductor rehearse and picking up snippets from the players backstage. Sometimes you get a feeling that a concert will be special right from the start. Last year's Martha Argerich concert had an astonishing atmosphere. It was the first time the San Francisco Symphony had ever played at the Proms, so there was an extra frisson in the orchestra. Add the cameras to that and you had real magic.' But even such triumphs can cause unsuspected challenges for a presenter: 'The reception Argerich got was so overwhelming that I had real problems – the roar of 5,000 voices is pretty difficult to talk over!'

After so many Proms, Stephanie has built up a rapport with the regular Prommers. 'At last year's Last Night

the crew had difficulty feeding the mike through my dress. I collapsed with laughter. The next thing I heard was the Prommers chanting "Arena to Stephanie: are you ticklish?".'

Audiences aren't always so friendly. 'Sometimes there's a long delay between pieces and people stare at you as if it's your link that's holding things up. But more often than not it's because a performer wants to comb their hair again or the concert manager suddenly realises that a score hasn't been put out.'

Yet, for Stephanie Hughes, nothing beats the magic of the Proms. 'In those

few seconds when you are preparing to go on air, and you hear the announcer back in the studio finishing off *In Tune*, and then you hear the mix in the box fading into the atmosphere in the hall, you think "This is it!" It's a wonderful moment. Off we go …'

Proms on Television

The following Proms will be shown live on **BBC2**: Prom 1, Prom 16, Prom 29 (*Turangalîla* only), Prom 49, Prom 71, Prom 73 (The Last Night: first half on BBC2, second half on BBC1)

The following Proms will be recorded for later transmission on **BBC1**: Prom 21, Prom 27, Prom 42, Prom 53

The following Proms will be shown on **BBC Knowledge**: Prom 11 (recorded), Proms 12–14 (live), Proms 17–18 (live)

BBC Proms Guide 2001

Published by BBC Proms Publications.
Editorial Office: Room 4084, Broadcasting House, Portland Place, London W1A 1AA
Distributed by BBC Worldwide, 80 Wood Lane, London W12 0TT

Editor: Mark Pappenheim
Publications Manager: Sarah Breeden
Editorial Manager: David Threasher
Publications Officer: Suzanne Esdell
Publications Assistant: Joanne Olagboyega

Design: Premm Design, London
Cover illustration: Brian Grimwood
Advertising: Cabbell Publishing Ltd, London
Printed by Garden House Press, London

© BBC 2001
ISBN 0–563–53433–8

BBC Proms 2001

Director: Nicholas Kenyon, Controller, BBC Proms, Live Events and TV Classical Music
Personal Assistant: Yvette Pusey
Artistic Administrator: Rosemary Gent
Concerts Administrator: Helen Burridge
Marketing Manager: Kate Finch
Business Assistant: Andrew King
Executive Producer, BBC Radio 3: Edward Blakeman

Leeds College of
Music

The College provides full and part-time courses including Indian Music, Western Music, Jazz, Contemporary Music and Music Technology – from DJ skills to instrument manufacture and repair. Courses range from post-16 education to degrees and postgraduate degrees.

Please contact us for further information and a copy of the prospectus.
Leeds College of Music
3 Quarry Hill, Leeds LS2 7PD
Telephone: 0113 222 3400
E-mail: enquiries@lcm.ac.uk
Web: www.lcm.ac.uk

Leeds
College of
Music

NEWARK & SHERWOOD COLLEGE
Newark School of Violinmaking

Further information contact:
01636 680680
or
mhunt@newark.ac.uk

Other Courses

Guitar Making
Piano Tuning
Lute Making
Instrument Making

Friary Road
Newark
Notts
NG24 1PB

Newark School
of
Violinmaking

www.violinmaking.co.uk

Index of Artists

Bold italic figures refer to Prom numbers
(PCM indicates Proms Chamber Music concerts: see pages 110–11).
* First appearance at a BBC Henry Wood Promenade Concert

Index of Works

Bold italic figures refer to Prom numbers
(PCM indicates Proms Chamber Music concerts:
see pages 110–11).
* First performance at a BBC Henry Wood
Promenade Concert

TEN OUT OF
TEN

With its enviable position and spectacular views over Hyde Park, The Tenth is one of London's finest restaurants.

ROYAL GARDEN HOTEL
LONDON

2-24 KENSINGTON HIGH STREET   LONDON W8 4PT
TELEPHONE 020 7937 8000   FAX 020 7361 1991
www.royalgardenhotel.co.uk